CHARLES DICKENS:
GREAT EXPECTATIONS

by

R. GEORGE THOMAS

Senior Lecturer in English,
University College, Cardiff

EDWARD ARNOLD (PUBLISHERS) LTD.
41 Maddox Street, London W1

Printed in Great Britain by
The Camelot Press Ltd., London and Southampton

General Preface

It has become increasingly clear in recent years that what both the advanced sixth former and the university student need most by way of help in their literary studies are close critical analyses and evaluations of individual works. Generalisations about periods or authors, general chat about the Augustan Age or the Romantic Movement, have their uses; but often they provide merely the illusion of knowledge and understanding of literature. All too often students come up to the university under the impression that what is required of them in their English literature courses is the referring of particular works to the appropriate generalisations about the writer or his period. Without taking up the anti-historical position of some of the American 'New Critics', we can nevertheless recognise the need for critical studies that concentrate on the work of literary art rather than on its historical background or cultural environment.

The present series is therefore designed to provide studies of individual plays, novels and groups of poems and essays, which are known to be widely studied in Sixth Forms and in universities. The emphasis is on clarification and evaluation; biographical and historical facts, while they may of course be referred to as helpful to an understanding of particular elements in a writer's work, will be subordinated to critical discussion. What kind of work is this? What exactly goes on here? How good is this work, and why? These are the questions which each writer will try to answer.

DAVID DAICHES

STUDIES IN ENGLISH LITERATURE No. 19

General Editor

David Daiches

Dean of the School of English and American Studies,
University of Sussex

For Edward G. Cox
and E. C. Llewellyn

Contents

Introductory

Great Expectations first appeared in weekly parts in Dickens's second periodical, *All the Year Round*; it ran from December 1860 until June 1861 and was subsequently issued in three volumes in the autumn of 1861, a few weeks before Dickens set out on his second tour of public readings from his works. Like *A Tale of Two Cities*, which also appeared in *All the Year Round*, *Great Expectations* is about two-thirds of the length of the other major novels, all of which were designed for monthly publication in twenty parts before they were issued as single works. Neither the weekly serial nor the first three-volume edition of *Great Expectations* was illustrated. Yet another distinguishing mark, which it also shares with *A Tale of Two Cities*, is the absence of any detailed memoranda about the novel's progress. Beginning with *Martin Chuzzlewit*, the initial composition of which had caused him considerable trouble and which marks the end of his first period of copious and felicitous writing, Dickens paid more attention to the forward planning of his novels and kept notes (still extant) in order 'to keep a steadier eye upon the general purpose and design'. There are no sketch notes for any individual numbers of *Great Expectations*; the notes which survive contain some detailed calculations about the ages of the ten chief characters, a calculation on the state of the tides on the Thames, and a sketch of the conclusion of the novel. These notes were drawn up after Chapter 42 (the story of Magwitch's life) was written and were designed to cover the last six chapters of the novel. They certainly throw no light on the original pattern of the story, although they give ample illustration of the firm measure of planned control which Dickens exercised over his tale. These notes also remind us of some of the difficulties inherent in the method of serial publication and of the special problem that often faced Dickens in rounding off his novels: a subject that cannot be avoided in discussing *Great Expectations* for which two endings were provided.

Fortunately John Forster, the novelist's friend, adviser, and correspondent, has recorded the genesis of the novel in some detail in *The Life of Charles Dickens*. In October 1860, Forster suggested that Dickens should 'let himself loose upon some single humorous conception in the vein of his youthful achievements in that way'. Relevant extracts from Dickens's replies made the next week are as follows:

'For a little piece I have been writing—or am writing; for I hope to finish it today—such a very fine, new, and grotesque idea has opened upon me, that I begin to doubt whether I had not better cancel the little paper and reserve the notion for a new book. You shall judge as soon as I get it printed. But it so opens out before *me* that I can see the whole of a serial revolving on it, in a most singular and comic manner.

'Last week I got to work on the new story. I had previously very carefully considered the state and prospects of *All the Year Round*, and, the more I considered them, the less hope I saw of being able to get back, now, to the profit of a separate publication [i.e. of *Great Expectations*] in the old 20 numbers. . . . I have therefore decided to begin the story as of the length of the *Tale of Two Cities* on the first of December— begin publishing, that is. I must make the most I can out of the book. You shall have the first two or three weekly parts tomorrow. The name is GREAT EXPECTATIONS. I think a good name?

'The book will be written in the first person throughout, and during these first three weekly numbers you will find the hero to be a boy-child, like David. I have made the opening, I hope, in its general effect exceedingly droll. I have put a child and a good-natured foolish man, in relations that seem to me very funny. Of course I have got in the pivot on which the story will turn too—and which indeed, as you remember, was the grotesque tragi-comic conception that first encouraged me. To be quite sure I had fallen into no unconscious repetitions, I read *David Copperfield* again the other day, and was affected by it to a degree you would hardly believe.

'It is a pity that the third portion [i.e. from Chapter 40 of the novel] cannot be read all at once, because its purpose would be much more apparent; and the pity is the greater, because the general turn and tone of the working out and winding up, will be away from all such things as they conventionally go. But what must be, must be. As to the planning out from week to week, nobody can imagine what the difficulty is, without trying. But, as in all such cases, when it is overcome the pleasure is proportionate. Two months more will see me through it, I trust. All the iron is in the fire, and I have "only" to beat it out.

'You will be surprised to hear that I have changed the end of *Great Expectations* from and after Pip's return to Joe's, and finding his little likeness there. Bulwer [Lytton], who has been, as I think you know, extraordinarily taken by the book, so strongly urged it upon me, after reading the proofs, and supported his view with such good reasons, that I resolved to make the change. You shall have it when you come back to town. I have put in as pretty a little piece of writing as I could, and I have no doubt the story will be more acceptable through the alteration.'

When *Great Expectations* was written Dickens was a very rich man but the novel does not give a rosy picture of a life of wealth. The middle fifties of the nineteenth century were critical years for Dickens's social thinking and this novel followed *Dombey and Son, Bleak House, Little Dorrit* and *Our Mutual Friend* in which Dickens tried 'with increasing success to create a vivid vision of society that would be at once extensive and comprehensive'. (Monroe Engel, *The Maturity of Dickens,* 1959.) Engel sees a difference in tone and approach between the two novels in which Dickens explored his 'sense of self', *David Copperfield* (1850) and *Great Expectations* ten years later: the former is a success story told in such a way that the pathos of the upward struggle of David remains uppermost in the reader's mind; whereas *Great Expectations* describes 'a movement away from success, and its dominant mood is ironic'. Though I agree with the view that *David Copperfield* is closer to our fuller understanding of Dickens's inner life than most of his novels, my many readings of *Great Expectations* have confirmed me in the opinion that the later novel is almost a model paradigm of Dickens's powerful response to the needs and aspirations of his own reading public. This later novel was written between the first and second of the novelist's lecture tours during which he read from his writings to large audiences and first tasted the power of his personal magnetism over crowds of devoted admirers. There is a sense in which Dickens has succeeded in *Great Expectations* in recapturing the lost art of the Icelandic writers of the Family Sagas—their ability 'to make books talk'. And though the analyses that follow in this study will try to lay bare the raw material and the varied techniques out of which Pip's story was constructed, this abiding sense of the uniform voice of the narrator (or is it the author?) remains once the novel is picked up and read through for enjoyment alone.

1. The Story, Plot, or Fable

Great Expectations was originally conceived as a 'grotesque, tragi-comic', long short-story. Very quickly, and in answer to the obvious need for a popular serial that would increase the falling sales of *All the Year Round*, it developed into a serial of weekly instalments that fully satisfied the taste of Dickens's weekly readers. In addition, this hastily expanded novel strengthened Dickens's standing as a novelist among the more critical readers of his day. Carlyle, it is true, thought it worth 'a penny to read before going to bed' and thoroughly enjoyed 'that Pip nonsense' which had sent him into roars of laughter. An anonymous reviewer in the *Saturday Review*, who had severely attacked some earlier novels, recognised that with *Great Expectations* Dickens had returned to his best vein, as exemplified by *Martin Chuzzlewit* and *David Copperfield*.

During the ten years before 1860, Dickens, as well as his critics, appeared to be more conscious of the technique of novel-writing and *Great Expectations* benefits considerably from a tighter plot-contrivance and a more closely organised and interwoven structure, than, say, *Pickwick Papers* or *Oliver Twist*.

The major structural feature of the novel is its division into the three distinct 'stages of Pip's Expectations'. The use of the word 'stage' is itself a suggestive one: it combines the notion of stages on a journey—so essential to any understanding of the pre-twentieth-century novel—with a suggestion of the theatre. Pip's progress from industrious obscurity, through wilful public idleness, to a resigned, yet modest acceptance of his true place in society is an obvious variation on the picaresque theme and carries with it many of the significant overtones of earlier picaresque novels. His progress, however, is rounded and compressed within three acts with a tightness of structure and a closeness of cross-reference that were rarely found in the private theatricals that then occupied Dickens's leisure. The clearest parallels to this dramatic division can be found in the novels of Jane Austen and in *Wuthering Heights*.

Dickens appears to be very conscious of the need to 'bring down the curtain' at the end of each 'stage' with a significant piece of writing. His sense of theatre was highly developed; the need for a flourish would have come very easily to him: Stage One ends (Chapter 19) with a faint suggestion of Adam and Eve leaving the Garden of Eden:

'We changed again, and yet again, and it was now too late and too far to go back, and I went on. And the mists had all solemnly risen now, and the world lay spread before me.'[1]

The penultimate paragraph is even more skilfully contrived as a running commentary on the state of the 'action' at this final moment in the first act:

'So subdued I was by those tears, and by their breaking out again in the course of the quiet walk, that when I was on the coach, and it was clear of the town, I deliberated with an aching heart whether I would not get down when we changed horses and walk back, and have another evening at home, and a better parting. We changed, and I had not made up my mind, and still reflected for my comfort that it would be quite practicable to get down and walk back, when we changed again. And while I was occupied with those deliberations, I would fancy an exact resemblance to Joe in some man coming along the road towards us, and my heart would beat high.—As if he could possibly be there!' As we read, the adult Pip, the narrator, is forgotten; probably because the contrasting ideas of forward motion and retrogression are sharply emphasised in the verbs. The desire to 'get down and walk back' is closely linked both with the word 'change' and the fanciful idea that Joe is walking out of the past to meet Pip at this decisive stage in his expectations. And then suddenly the narrator takes charge in the continuous present tense ('As if he could possibly be there!') and terminates the moment of hesitancy. The final paragraph brings down the curtain with an echo of the 'mists that were solemnly rising' when Pip had left the village where he 'had been so innocent'.

The end of the second stage of Pip's expectations (Chapter 39) is described in nine short paragraphs. They are designed to sum up the entire action of the novel (in so far as it concerns Pip's inner biography) up to this point when the curtain is lowered on this moment of despair and ruin in his fortunes: 'the clocks of the Eastward churches were striking five, the candles were wasted out, the fire was dead, and the wind and rain intensified the thick black darkness'. The passage is skilfully contrived. Pip and Magwitch are cut off from the world like two

---

[1] All quotations from the novel are taken from *Great Expectations*, The New Oxford Illustrated Dickens, 1953.

characters imprisoned within a stage set. The shutters are drawn and communication with all other characters is at an end; Magwitch brings into the room all the old eating habits of the escaped convict until Pip is left up centre stage with his memories of Miss Havisham, Estella, the Old Bailey, Herbert, Joe and Biddy. Even a <u>faint suggestion of super-natural promptings and forebodings are given in order to emphasise Pip's loneliness and sense of isolation</u>: 'With these fears upon me, I began either to imagine or recall that I had had mysterious warnings of this man's approach. . . . That, his wicked spirit had somehow sent these messengers to mine, and that now on this stormy night he was as good as his word, and with me.' Pip's final attempt to break the tension of his bad dream by taking one last look at his 'dreadful burden' has its own theatrical quality and the sleeping ex-convict is presented to the reader in the close-up manner of Dickens's usual reliance on vividly detailed description: 'He had rolled a handkerchief round his head, and his face was set and lowering in his sleep.' <u>Inevitably, and melodramat-ically,</u> 'he had a pistol lying on the pillow'.

Professors John Butt and Kathleen Tillotson have noted that Dickens experienced considerable difficulty in writing some of the last double numbers which concluded his monthly instalments; his notebooks for *Dombey and Son, David Copperfield* and *Little Dorrit* are thick with jottings at this point. The notes for *Great Expectations* seem to have been written after Chapter 43 and were apparently designed to maintain the pattern of the story unchanged throughout the last six chapters. Leaving aside for the present any discussion of the alternative endings and accepting the end as Dickens published it, we can see that Dickens still thought of the ending of this third and final stage in theatrical terms. All the minor characters are suitably paired off or dismissed from the action with a characteristic gesture: Satis House is pulled down; Herbert and Clara, like Biddy and Joe, are married; only the Blue Boar Inn, the Forge, the mist, the churchyard, and the deserted garden remain unchanged and unaltered. The marshes, the hulks, the traces and echoes of crime and punishment are replaced by the newly emerging life of another young Pip and the final, subdued meeting of Pip and Estella. In echoic fashion, the third stage—this time a stage on a journey that will continue after the novel is ended—recaptures the mood and the terms of reference of the end of the first stage of Pip's expectations:

'I took her hand in mine, and we went out of the ruined place; and, as the morning mists had risen long ago when I first left the forge, so, the evening mists were rising now, and in all the broad expanse of tranquil light they showed to me, I saw no shadow of another parting from her.'

Theatrical methods are also used by Dickens in the main body of his narrative. In all his novels he relies on set scenes that are almost ready to be transported to the stage. During the last decade Mr. Emlyn Williams, following Dickens's own example on his successful reading tours, has demonstrated the ease with which selected scenes from the novels can yield the raw material for a whole evening's entertainment in the theatre. *Great Expectations* abounds in such potentially 'dramatic sketches' between two speakers.

In the majority of instances these scenes are brief: Pip and the convict (Chapter 3), Pip and Joe (7); Joe, his wife, and Orlick (15); Mr. Wopsle and Mr. Jaggers (18). But occasionally in the later part of the novel such stage scenes are extended in scope, range and dramatic intensity until the reader can imagine that he is sitting in the wings or is present at a dress rehearsal. There are two memorable scenes of this nature. In Chapter 38 Pip's dreams of wealth and expectation are about to collapse with the return of Magwitch. One shaky prop in this fanciful super-structure was his belief that Estella would eventually become his wife. The entire chapter is designed to destroy this illusion and to force Pip to see through both the character of Miss Havisham and the uncertain foundations for his own wild dreams. His moment of revelation is first presented to the reader as autobiographical recollection:

'I saw in this, wretched though it made me, and bitter the sense of dependence, even of degradation, that it awakened—I saw in this, that Estella was set to wreak Miss Havisham's revenge on men, and that she was not to be given to me until she had gratified it for a term I saw in this, a reason for her being beforehand assigned to me. Sending her out to attract and torment and do mischief, Miss Havisham sent her with the malicious assurance that she was beyond the reach of all admirers, and that all who staked upon that cast were secured to lose. I saw in this, that I, too, was tormented by a perversion of ingenuity, even while the prize was reserved for me. I saw in this, the reason for my being staved off so long, and the reason for my late guardian's declining to commit himself to the formal knowledge of such a scheme. In a word, I saw in this, Miss Havisham as I had her then and there before my eyes, and always had had her before my eyes; and I saw in this, the distinct shadow of the darkened and unhealthy house in which her life was hidden from the sun.

'The candles that lighted that room of hers were placed in sconces on the wall. They were high from the ground, and they burnt with the steady dullness of artificial light in air that is seldom renewed. As I looked round at them, and at the pale gloom they made, and at the stopped clock, and at the withered articles of bridal dress upon the table and the ground, and at her own awful figure with its ghostly reflection thrown large by the fire upon the ceiling and the wall, I saw in everything the construction that my mind had come to, repeated and thrown back to me. My thoughts passed into the great room across the landing where the table was spread, and I saw it written, as it were, in the falls of the cobwebs from the centrepiece, in the crawlings of the spiders on the cloth, in the tracks of the mice as they betook their little quickened hearts behind the panels, and in the gropings and pausings of the beetles on the floor.'

So far Dickens relies heavily on the visual recreation of the details of the seen (e.g. the repetition of 'I saw'); but as Pip continues to stare at the two women, the scene becomes a theatre and the tensions inherent in the relationship between them are brought to a verbal climax in the following dialogue:

' "Did I never give her love!" cried Miss Havisham, turning wildly to me. "Did I never give her a burning love, inseparable from jealousy at all times, and from sharp pain, while she speaks thus to me! Let her call me mad, let her call me mad!"

' "Why should I call you mad," returned Estella, "I, of all people? Does any one live, who knows what set purposes you have, half as well as I do? Does any one live, who knows what a steady memory you have, half as well as I do? I who have sat on this same hearth on the little stool that is even now beside you there, learning your lessons and looking up into your face, when your face was strange and frightened me!"

' "Soon forgotten!" moaned Miss Havisham. "Times soon forgotten!"

' "No, not forgotten," retorted Estella. "Not forgotten, but treasured up in my memory. When have you found me false to your teaching? When have you found me unmindful of your lessons? When have you

B

found me giving admission here," she touched her bosom with her hand, "to anything that you excluded? Be just to me."

' "So proud, so proud!" moaned Miss Havisham, pushing away her grey hair with both her hands.

' "Who taught me to be proud?" returned Estella. "Who praised me when I learnt my lesson?"

' "So hard, so hard!" moaned Miss Havisham, with her former action.

' "Who taught me to be hard?" returned Estella. "Who praised me when I learnt my lesson?"

' "But to be proud and hard to *me*!" Miss Havisham quite shrieked, as she stretched out her arms. "Estella, Estella, Estella, to be proud and hard to *me*!"

'Estella looked at her for a moment with a kind of calm wonder, but was not otherwise disturbed; when the moment was passed, she looked down at the fire again.

' "I cannot think," said Estella, raising her eyes after a silence, "why you should be so unreasonable when I come to see you after a separation. I have never forgotten your wrongs and their causes. I have never been unfaithful to you or your schooling. I have never shown any weakness that I can charge myself with."

' "Would it be weakness to return my love?" exclaimed Miss Havisham. "But yes, yes, she would call it so!"

' "I begin to think," said Estella, in a musing way, after another moment of calm wonder, "that I almost understand how this comes about. If you had brought up your adopted daughter wholly in the dark confinement of these rooms, and had never let her know that there was such a thing as the daylight by which she has never once seen your face—if you had done that, and then, for a purpose, had wanted her to understand the daylight and know all about it, you would have been disappointed and angry?"

'Miss Havisham, with her head in her hands, sat making a low moaning, and swaying herself on her chair, but gave no answer.

' "Or," said Estella, "—which is a nearer case—if you had taught her, from the dawn of her intelligence, with your utmost energy and might, that there was such a thing as daylight, but that it was made to be her enemy and destroyer, and she must always turn against it, for it had blighted you and would else blight her;—if you had done this, and then, for a purpose, had wanted her to take naturally to the daylight and she could not do it, you would have been disappointed and angry?"

'Miss Havisham sat listening (or it seemed so, for I could not see her face), but still made no answer.

' "So," said Estella, "I must be taken as I have been made. The success is not mine, the failure is not mine, but the two together make me." '

As the scene ends Pip decides to leave the room and, as he looks back, we are supplied with a final view of the stage set as the curtain comes down: 'When I left, Estella was yet standing by the great chimney-piece, just as she had stood throughout. Miss Havisham's grey hair was all adrift upon the ground, among the other bridal wrecks, and was a miserable sight to see.'

The second scene of extended stage dialogue is in Chapter 50, when Herbert informs Pip of Provis's story about his child. The entire chapter —a very short one—shows quite clearly that Dickens was in complete control of his narrative. Pip's hands and arms are bandaged after the fire at Satis House and in the first two paragraphs the reader's attention is directed toward's Pip's acute suffering. When he dozes off the details of the fire are recalled vividly, in his dreams; when he awakens, the unspoken problem of Provis's safety is hinted at. 'But then, as Herbert changed the bandages, more by the light of the fire than by the outer light, he went back to it spontaneously. "I sat with Provis last night, Handel, two good hours." ' The stage has been set—even the lighting has been suggested—and the dialogue continues for three pages until the rather melodramatic last line is spoken by Pip:

' "I know I am quite myself. And the man we have in hiding down the river is Estella's Father." '

There is no need to illustrate the point further, but the student will find for himself at least a dozen other scenes in the novel—including nearly all those which involve Mr. Jaggers—that demonstrate Dickens' constant reliance on such theatrical set pieces both to enliven the flow of his narrative and to concentrate the moments of high tension into memorable dialogue.

Great Expectations illustrates no single theory of narrative construction. Dickens employs a mixed form which embraces the best qualities and methods found in the practice of earlier novelists and in his own earlier successful novels. The ingredients are many and varied, but no set recipe emerges. Dickens's earlier exuberance of comic invention, both in situation and dialogue, is now less spontaneous and this is to be expected from so prolific a writer and public speaker. Yet at no time did the fountain of humour run dry and in *Great Expectations* the comic scenes are successfully integrated into the general purpose of the story. There is some difference in their employment between the first 'stage' and the other two, and many characters (e.g. Pumblechook, Wopsle and, to some extent, Wemmick) undergo a subtle change as the novel progresses. Conceived originally, one suspects, in the Pickwickian fantastic sense, the comic characters are later used to further the story, to unravel entanglements in the plot, or even to round out the many half-hidden themes that lie just below the surface of the plain narrative. A few set-pieces remain: Pip's sister 'on the Rampage'; Mr. Wopsle's reading of *George Barnwell* (Chapter 15); Mr. Pumblechook's 'May I' (Chapter 19); Pip's introduction to the family of Mr. Matthew Pocket (Chapters 22, 23); the behaviour of Trabb's boy (Chapter 30); and some of the encounters at Walworth with, as a final *tour de force*, the wedding of Wemmick and Miss Skiffins (Chapter 55). Such comic scenes, which are developed solely for their own intrinsic comic worth, become rarer as the story advances towards its climax. Wemmick disappears from the novel one chapter before Magwitch dies and, as the story returns more closely to its village origins, Joe and Pumblechook are left to supply the comedy in a slightly altered key.

A third and vestigial narrative method employed in the novel is the 'inset story' which was so frequently used by those eighteenth-century novelists which the young Dickens had read so eagerly. The most significant is Magwitch's story of his life (Chapter 42). Despite the 'low' style in which it is narrated, Magwitch's story ('put at once into a mouthful of English') is a *reductio ad absurdum* of all the picaresque tales ever told in English or French novels: 'In jail and out of jail, in jail and out of jail, in jail and out of jail.' But this is no mere device adopted by Dickens mechanically or unthinkingly. In *Great Expectations* the numerous flash-back narratives certainly clarify some of the mysteries inherent in the plot; they also help to thicken the sense of 'time past' converging upon and dominating 'time present'. The device is absorbed into the thematic as well as the structural pattern of the autobiography or *Bildungsroman*. As the third 'stage' is unfolded before him, the reader becomes conscious of the consummate skill with which the narrator is re-living the past as he tells it. In this carefully organised approach to a unitary narrative, the 'inset-tales' are utilised to give the sense of pre-destined events that somehow condition Pip's behaviour without excusing it. The approach to the past is impersonal and our attention is concentrated upon the events; we react to the fate of the teller at a distance which is one remove from the incidents themselves, which are filtered through to us by hindsight and retrospection. By contrast, the barbarous dialect which Dickens puts into Magwitch's mouth, and the occasional descriptions of his coarse manners which interrupt the narrative, help to concentrate our attention on Magwitch not only as he lived through these long past events but also as they have affected the rest of his life. Dickens is employing a double perspective and, in the process, he brings the climax of his tale one step nearer and makes it more credible. When the narrative is over, the reader has shared, if only temporarily, the convict's ingrained hatred for Compeyson. The barbarous fight in the ditch (from Chapter 5) invades the upper room in Barnard's Inn where the two young city gentlemen are listening and casts its shadow forward towards the locked death-struggle with Compeyson in the Thames at the end of Chapter 54. In seven pages Dickens has tightened the threads of his narrative, darkened the easy-going life of two young men with memories of a world quite distinct from their own, and released into the drawing-room, dream-like world of Pip's second 'stage' those pent-up forces of the picaro life of rogues and vagabonds which lie below and just beyond the pale of respectable organised society and which, at any moment of crisis, threaten to rise and destroy it. Carlyle, the historian of the French Revolution, may have laughed at that 'Pip nonsense'; Magwitch's life-story darkens the nonsense with overtones from *A Tale of Two Cities* and the underworld of Victorian London.

The structural patterns in *Great Expectations* have been analysed in some detail by John H. Hagan (*E.L.H.*, XXI, 1; 1954). After referring to the most conspicuous artistry with which 'the story has been organised into three large sections of virtually equal length' which correspond in 'moral or temporal terms' to phases of Boyhood, Youth and Maturity, Mr. Hagan points out that each one of the stages 'has its various subdivisions, no less evident because they go without explicit mention'. Stage One is divided into four subdivisions: Chapters 1-6, 7-11, 12-17 and 18-19. Stage Two's subdivisions are Chapters 20-27, 28-35, and

36-39; those for Stage Three are Chapters 40-46, 47-51, 52-56 and 57-59. Consciously, or unconsciously, Dickens has imposed on his novel a balancing external appearance of symmetry which becomes even more significant when the various subdivisions are regarded as reflecting images balanced around the central point of the narrative. Mr. Hagan's analysis should be read in full but the following examples will suggest the nature of his argument. Chapters 1-6 contain Pip's first encounter with the convict; Chapters 40-46 are devoted to their second meeting; Chapters 7-11, in which Pip is first introduced to Miss Havisham and Estella, are balanced against Chapters 47-51 where Miss Havisham's nature begins to alter and Estella's parentage is revealed; Pip's departure from the old Forge (Chapters 18-19) is balanced by his return there as an experienced, disillusioned man in Chapters 57-59. In other words, each subdivision in the first Stage of Pip's expectations is balanced, fulfilled and completed by the corresponding section in the third Stage.

This is no mere act of mechanical balancing. The successive stages in the growth of Pip's expectations develop gradually but perceptibly from Pip's own acts of deceit. He lies about the file and the food out of terror and sheer fright, but his fanciful embroidering of his visit to Satis House is a conscious and calculated act of deception with deep roots in snobbery and class-consciousness. From this moment onwards the graph of his own capacity for self-deceit can be easily drawn until it culminates in the advent of Jaggers and the fortuitous connection between Miss Havisham, Pip, Jaggers and the 'great expectations'. But, even then, all the links in this hidden chain of chance, deceit, circum-spection, hypocrisy, snobbery, crime and mania have not been fully uncovered. With sure skill and fine economy Dickens advances his story within a vast interlocking series of events that must wait upon time, memory, recollection and revelation before their unseen tangles are made clear in the last and third Stage. Pip's rise to a position of unstable prosperity, balanced as it was on a series of progressive acts of self-deceit, is counterbalanced by his final return to the workaday world of hard work and honest reward which is achieved through a series of acts of clear vision and knowledge not only about his own nature but also about all the characters who have come to form the society in which he lives out his life of easy expectancy.

In retrospect one is surprised at the small number of minor characters in the novel and even more surprised at the even smaller number who have no connection at all with the main story except at one point. The careful balancing of incident between the first and third Stages is paralleled in the multiple functions of secondary characters like Wopsle, Orlick, Drummle, Startop and Pumblechook who double up their parts with the same skill—and, perhaps, the same show of contrivance— that characterises Mr. Wopsle's theatrical performances in London. Eventually, of course, the number of actors is reduced until the intimate circle of Joe, Mrs. Joe and Pip is re-created in the home of Joe, Biddy and *their* child, Pip, who is no longer an orphan but the happy offspring of a genuine marriage of affection.

Enough has been said—though one tithe of the possible illustration of these repetitive patterns has been used above—to suggest the close fidelity with which Dickens has organised his plot material around a few central ideas and incidents. It would be a gross misrepresentation of the novel's scope to maintain that anything like a fraction of Pip's expectations are ever realised in terms of narrative adventure, width of scene, or breadth of social intercourse. The social boundaries of the novel are quite narrow. Estella and Drummle, Mrs. Pocket and Mrs. Brandley, supply faint lines of communication to a slightly more genteel world than that of Pumblechook and Wemmick; the locale of the rest of the novel is shadowy and ill-defined, except where it is fantastic, sordid or rural. Nor, except for the sudden spurts of action as the climax approaches, is the action of the story carried forward on the open, classless road so beloved by Smollett and Fielding. There are still a few carefully observed road journeys in *Great Expectations* and, offstage, we are informed of the wanderings of Magwitch and Compeyson, Provis's life in Australia, and the activities of Clarriker and Co. 'in the East', but my residual memory of the story is of long journeys on foot interspersed with the sudden culminating incidents on the Thames. By confining the social and spatial boundaries of his story, Dickens was left free to explore Pip's memories in depth—particularly those half-recollected depths of memory that rise, at first, haphazardly to the surface of consciousness before the full flood of more detailed, interconnected incidents can lay bare the springs of conduct and choice. Any close analysis of the novel's structure may possibly give the impression that Dickens has manipulated his plot to good effect. This is not the impression left by a re-reading of the novel: it has a thoroughly satisfying sense of rounded completeness and organic unity.

Dickens was not careless about the treatment of time in *Great Expectations*. (As we have seen above, his few extant notes about the novel contain much about the ages of his chief characters.) Like Scott, Thackeray, George Eliot and the Brontës, Dickens tried to set the action of most of his novels vaguely within living memory and although, as Humphrey House and others have pointed out, he was not always careful in his back-dating, his addiction to the Age of the Coach (just prior to the Railway Age) freed his novels from any suggestion of a distant, romantic past while allowing to the novelist a free hand in the invention of realistic and verifiable settings. Miss Mary Edminson has shown ('The Date of the Action of *Great Expectations*', *N.C.F.*, XIII, 1958) that the main action of this novel is established 'within a definite period, with great care'. The convicts' hulks were condemned in 1847; Pip uses flint and steel (before the first 'lucifer' was invented in 1827) when he was 7 years old; in Chapter 46 there is a reference to the Old London Bridge which was finally replaced in August 1831, so that Pip was 23 some time before that date; Wemmick's Catalogue of six Bridges (Chapter 36) contains none opened after 1819 so that Pip cannot be 21 before 1819; two references, to paddle steamers (Chapter 54) and to the restricted use of steam navigation before the early 1840s, suggest a date for the attempted escape abroad with Magwitch at a time close to 1824. Miss Edminson's evidence indicates that the main action of the story was enacted between 1807 (or 1810) and 1823 (or 1826). Many other details, woven almost casually into the text, support this assumption. On his return Magwitch is dressed in 'shorts', a slang term for breeches that went out of fashion around 1815; gas light was introduced in 1807 but was not in general use before the period 1814-20; transportation to New South Wales was discontinued in 1840. In fact, Dickens was as consistent about the temporal setting of the action as he was about the internal dating and causal relationships of the internal action of his story. He appears to have taken great pains to remove his story from the area of contemporary observation—if not of possible living memory—and so to concentrate any social criticism implicit in his tale against the more timeless defects in human society which arise when moral values and social aspirations have gone astray.

More pertinently for any analysis of the structure of *Great Expectations* is the validity with which this careful temporal setting invests the auto-biographical recollections of Pip the narrator whose story we are reading. If we can trust Pip's recollection of things past when his word can be checked against folk-memory or historical records, then surely— we are forced to conclude—we may accept him as a reasonably honest and reliable interpreter of his own feelings and attitudes towards the highly personal, introspective actions that he records. Dickens re-read *David Copperfield* as Pip's story was being shaped in order to avoid unnecessary plagiarism or repetition. We also know that David's tale often comes very close to Dickens's own autobiography: indeed, large sections of the earlier novel are so compulsively written that the reader can neither put it down nor fail to hear the very voice of the author (narrator) speaking. There is none of this attention-compelling prose in Pip's recollections; instead we accept its cool veracity and follow the narration with a genuine, yet uncommitted concern for the outcome of events. We believe in them without being forcibly held by an Ancient-Mariner-like hypnosis. The difference between the two novels, in this respect at least, is a measure of Dickens's great care to ground Pip's life-story on externally verifiable facts that would cast an aura of truthfulness over the more imaginative (and personally tender) sections of the novel.

It would be surprising if Dickens's imposition of fixed temporal limits on Pip's story, however apposite a reflection of the narrator's very act of recollection it proved to be, were to result in a weakening of the sense of place within the novel as a whole.

A significant part of *Great Expectaions* is presented to us in dramatic scenes and in long snatches of dramatic dialogue, but not at the expense of the usual, detailed Dickensian description of the localities and 'sets' against which the action takes place. For, as George Orwell and others have emphasised, Dickens's imaginative reconstruction of the world of experience is marked by his close attention to observed details: his art, even at its most fantastic point, is an extension of his amazingly gifted reporter's eye. In other words, it is impossible to imagine a novel by Dickens, however controlled and centrally organised in the service of a single dominating theme, that does not pay close attention to the locale in which the action is carried out. So that just as the stage-like scenes and passages of rapid dialogue suspend the forward drive of the plot for a time, and incidentally provide moments of rest, the passages of set description can also give their own points of rest and timelessness within the framework of the fast-moving narrative. At such moments, for example the visits to Walworth or Newgate, the first introduction to the home of Matthew Pocket, the meeting with Drummle at the Blue Boar, the restless night spent at Hummums, the walk to Chinks's Basin along the Old Green Copper Rope-Walk, the taut scene at the Sessions, —and numerous other passages scattered throughout the novel—Dickens seems to be broadening his canvas rather than advancing his story. There is undoubtedly a fast-moving tale, carefully set in place and time, which takes place between Pip's seventh and twenty-third birthdays; there is also a sense in which the entire novel is constructed like a series of radiating spokes which move away from a single remembered experience and which are held in place and perspective by the fully-rounded circumferential knowledge of the mature Pip. And this knowledge is shared with the reader when the last stage of Pip's expectations is reached. In his perceptive study of 'Dickens and the Sense of Time' (*N.C.F.*, XIII, 1958), Mr. John H. Raleigh argues that in both *David Copperfield* and *Great Expectations* the 'idea of existence in time as a compound of memory and desire' is added to 'the temporal implications of the involved plotting'. Mr. Raleigh finds that generally in the novels of Dickens there are two plot lines: one on the surface and one which is either hinted at or completely submerged. Certainly, the care taken by Dickens to present acceptable times and places for *Great Expectations* arose from an instinct deeper than the serial plotter's desire for a superficial tidiness: his concern with the numerical aspects of time is paralleled by a wider concern with the place of chance, pre-destination and maturity in the life-patterns of his four principal characters, Pip, Estella, Magwitch and Miss Havisham.

Pip's story has many overtones precisely because the elements from so many different kinds of story-teller have gone into its telling. Sir Philip Sidney's apology for poetry can be extended to include Dickens's novel: 'If then a man can arrive, at that child's age to know that the poets' persons and doings are but pictures what should be, and not stories what have been, they will never give the lie to things not affirmatively but allegorically and figuratively written. And therefore, as in History looking for truth, they go away full fraught with falsehood, so in Poesy, looking for fiction, they shall use the narration but as an imaginative ground-plot of a profitable invention.' The imaginative ground-plot of *Great Expectations* is a fairy-tale adjusted to the taste and needs of the mature, adult mind: it caters for an adult sense of disillusionment with the haphazard gifts of Fortune and, at the same time, it feeds the subconscious desires and dreams of all men for a perfectionist world, an Earthly Paradise in which magic has its place and where transformation episodes (like Pip's change from the Forge to a gentleman) can really come to pass. For it is part of Dickens's strength as a novelist that, although his clear perception of certain social evils lies at the heart of his more sombre later novels, he never lost sight of the 'vision splendid'.

To achieve this double vision Dickens employed multiple and diverse techniques of story-telling. The majestically controlled account of Magwitch's final attempt at escape (Chapter 54) must be balanced against the melodramatic poverty of Orlick's attempted murder in the previous chapter; Miss Havisham's credible, psycho-pathological way of life must be accepted along with the rather shadowy life lived by Mr. Jaggers' ex-murderess housekeeper; one's rounded affection for Joe, as for someone in real life, is as much part of the novel as one's rather detached, tolerant, yet humorous acceptance of the way Dickens allows Wemmick, Aged P and Miss Skiffins to go through their Punch-and-Judy show for our delectation. The freedom and pace of genuine picaresque sequences are as essential to the novel as the stage-like scenes and the impassioned descriptions of time and place. A few sentimental passages, and one or two pieces of direct address to the reader, interrupt the flow of the narrative and jar on our contemporary sense of fitness in the reader-author relationship. But even these are caught up into the action of the story which never flags because at all times Dickens is either leading us onward with new incidents or filling in the outlines of what we already know. For *Great Expectations* is an admirable example of one of Lionel Trilling's many dicta about 'Manners, Morals and the Novel': 'The novel, then, is a perpetual quest for reality, the field of its research being always the social world, the material of its analysis being always manners as the indication of the direction of man's soul.'

2. Characterisation

Dickens, like Shakespeare, was a creator as well as an inheritor of the English language and many of the <u>identifiable catch-phrases</u> attached to his characters are known only at one remove from the novels as a phrase or a name. In this merely verbal sense Falstaff and Sarah Gamp, Oliver Twist's request and Malvolio's rebuke, Sidney Carton's dying words and Horatio's epitaph on Hamlet, all share the same kind of immortality. The obvious danger, then, is to allow the expected Dickensian qualities to blind us to the peculiar excellences and restraints of a particular novel, especially in a novel as well organised and as carefully executed as *Great Expectations*. This novel, too, has its catch-phrases and some of its characters are as comically grotesque as any that went before; but they are not exuberantly scattered throughout the story: with few exceptions they are made to serve the novelist's turn with the utmost economy.

Dickens has succeeded in integrating a considerable number of his minor, 'humorous' (in the Jonsonian sense) characters into the main stream of his novel: there are few failures. It is inevitable that Mrs. Joe should give up 'the Rampage' and cease to bring up anyone 'by hand' once she was murderously attacked, but even she continues a vicarious and posthumous existence in the many-sided use made of Pumblechook, who is revived time and time again throughout the story in order to act as a comic claque and to represent that quite common obtuseness of judgement that fails to recognise the change of character that takes place behind too-familiar faces. Trabb's boy is also resurrected for the sake of the story—and perhaps to hint at the unchanging quality of life in the small town—but a newly minted character could have served *his* turn. The soldiers at the beginning of the first Stage, like the Customs Officers and law men at the end of the story, the hangers-on in Little Britain, or the judge and jurors in the Court of Sessions, have the merest walking-on parts necessary for crowd scenes. This is the rôle, too, designed for the toadies at Satis House, for Mr. and Mrs. Hubble, for Mrs. Brandley of Richmond and, one must add regretfully, for Bill Barley and his gentle daughter, Clara.

Once these characters are introduced into the story Dickens seems compelled to bring them to some semblance of life. The *Uncommercial*

Traveller reveals quite plainly that Boz never lost his ear for <u>natural dialogue</u>—whether real or invented—nor his eye for the eccentric touches in scene, dress, figure or situation. In some of his earlier novels situations appear to have been invented in order to display the particular Bozian gifts at the expense of the narrative structure; on such occasions, one's dissatisfaction is not with his vital capacity to bring new characters to life but with his abandonment of them. There is little of this dissatisfaction in the characters mentioned above: Bill Barley is a welcome relief from the tense and sombre stretches of story that follow Magwitch's return; the sergeant and his soldiers at the Forge help to fill in time (and delay suspense) as functionally and successfully as the 'grizzled male creature, the "Jack" of the little causeway' does while Magwitch is making his last attempt at escape. Even Pumblechook's nauseating 'May I' strikes an acceptable note of the sycophancy which accompanies all sudden realisations of 'expectations'. But, then, Dickens persevered with Pumblechook and for some unknown reason abandoned Mrs. Belinda Pocket to oblivion after rounding out her snobbish pretensions to quite considerable proportions in one and a half chapters. There is no comparable dismissal in the entire novel.

The next group of characters to be considered are much more closely integrated into the accidental occurences that surround the centrally-placed fable of the rise and fall of Pip's good fortune. They are, in order of appearance—and almost of departure—Wopsle, Compeyson, Orlick, Herbert, Drummle, Startop and Wemmick (carrying with him the Aged Parent and that best of all portable properties, Miss Skiffins). Startop is the odd man out in this group: he is a shadowy creation, a necessary strong arm attached to an ordinary body, who is vital to the action at the climax of the play and, just possibly, a thematic foil to Drummle's pretensions. The other six characters contribute as much to the theme of the novel as they do to the action—if, indeed, the two aspects of the book's central design can be separated. Apart from his identification of Compeyson in the theatre, Wopsle follows his own fantastic dream of fame as surely as Pip does, but without any final disillusionment: his world of fantasy is as thin as the eighteenth-century play's projection of George Barnwell the London apprentice. Compeyson, like Drummle, is essential to the mechanics of the many-tiered plot and also shows up the basic unreality of Magwitch's assumption that 'being a gentleman' (by birth or through unearned wealth) is one of the best blessings he can bestow on the blacksmith's lad. Orlick is a grotesque creation: part ogre, part unrealised demon king from Pantomine, part Cain and, at times, part villain from the cheapest melodrama, he stalks through the marsh country and the dark fastnesses of the urban under-world like Grendel in the Old English poem *Beowulf*. His very name, though copied by Dickens from an authentic list, seems to mark him down for violence, shame and the gallows. He is a Caliban without the poetic speeches. The conception of Wemmick seems to grow under the novelist's pen as the novel proceeds. When he is first described to us (Chapter 21) we immediately recognise the Dickensian play of fancy reserved for a comic figure: 'I found him to be a dry man, rather short in stature, with a square wooden face, whose expression seemed to have been imperfectly chipped out with a dull-edged chisel. . . . His mouth was such a post-office of a mouth that he had a mechanical appearance of smiling . . .'. At Walworth he is fitted into a wooden miniature castle like a child's toy soldier and seems all set to become a necessary toy, a source for Dickens's bizarre image-making and no more. Quickly he is more closely identified with the central action of Provis's return and his function in the novel is enlarged. He plays a variety of parts and sounds many chords in the narrator's recollections. His suburban pastoral existence is manifestly inferior to life at the Forge; his two contrasting natures (at Walworth and Little Britain) are shrewd comments on the nature of work in a growing metropolis; his small-minded, yet realistic attitude to love and portable property is sharply contrasted with Pip's extravagances. He is a courier to Newgate and he supplies some clues to the gaps in the novel's pre-history. And yet so sure is Dickens's touch that despite these multifarious functions he remains throughout as the Wooden Wemmick whom we first meet in Chapter 21. Carlos Lynes (*Forms of Modern Fiction*, p. 185) discusses André Gide's refusal to 'follow through' his characters when they are first introduced to the reader because of his 'unwillingness to compromise the spontaneity of his future response by his present choice'. Dickens knows nothing of this unwillingness: he is quite prepared to allow Wemmick some spontaneous touches of 'human' affection. His cautious arm steals around Miss Skiffins's waist in order to provide touches of humour; his sudden outburst of compassion in Jaggers' office occurs at a critical moment in Pip's desperate search into the origins of Estella. But these are exceptional moments of liberation from the wooden frame inside which Dickens has placed him: he comes 'alive' when it suits the author and not in response to any spontaneous impulse of his own.

Two characters, Molly (housekeeper to Jaggers) and Matthew Pocket (father of Herbert, relative of Miss Havisham and tutor to Pip) are not easily assigned to any category: each plays a minor part in the story, neither is fully-drawn and yet together they add depth to the 'moral fable' that lies barely concealed beneath the tale of Pip's expectations. Neither character is completely visualised for the reader; while Matthew, in particular, could fit smoothly into the world of *Alice in Wonderland*, Molly could slip easily into the nightmare world of *The Woman in White*. The reader's portrait of each character is deduced from what they do (or have done) and not from any visual or verbal qualities which are imposed upon the reader's consciousness by the novelist. Fulfilling necessary rôles in the superficial plot, they are essentially allegorical personages. Matthew stands for many qualities which touch the quick of the moral problems raised by Pip's easy accession to wealth: improvidence, a gentlemanly ideal of education, an old-fashioned conception of honour, impracticability in the conduct of his career or his domestic life, etc. He is a Compeyson who has not gone wrong and for whom nothing has gone right. In contrast to his over-refined and ineffectually educated nature, Molly stands for the intuitive world of instincts and uncontrolled passions. The power of the law and of fear hold the maimed, almost animal-like creature in check; she represents forces inimical to society which might, at any moment, break loose and help to destroy it. Even more obviously than Matthew she belongs to the thematic, subconscious world of the novel; another addition to the crowded gallery of abnormal, maladjusted characters that exerted such a powerful fascination over Dickens's imagination.

All the remaining characters play a major part in the dramatic and thematic world of *Great Expectations*: Joe, Magwitch, Jaggers, Miss Havisham, Estella, Biddy and Herbert. Of these seven, the two last are the least significant: both are firmly embedded in the plot-structure of the narrative and each throws a clear light on the tale's central theme. Together with Estella and Pip they represent the younger generation that is operated upon by the designs, tyrannies and misjudgements of their elders. The essential continuing life of the novel—which moves beyond the terminal dates of the tale precisely because the novel's narrative technique leads one *à la recherche du temps perdu*—rests in their hands; when Miss Havisham has been consumed by fire and Magwitch has failed to survive his baptism in the waters of the Thames, the life of the novel still goes forward. Equally with the other major characters, Biddy and Herbert change under the novelist's hand as the story develops and the original, half-comic, grotesquely conceived plot is transformed into a critique of an acquisitive society. Biddy in the Dame's School is far removed (in conception, presentation and function) from the world of Estella; long before the novel ends she and Estella are presented to the reader, through the eyes and memory of Pip the narrator, as complementary aspects of desirable female nature. In contrast to Pip and Herbert, both young ladies know quite clearly what they wish to get out of life: the final resolution of Pip's love for Estella is supported by his (and our) understanding of Biddy's essentially sane acceptance of her rôle as a wife and mother. In similar fashion, Herbert begins his life as a comic foil to Pip, the blacksmith's boy, before he, too, is involved with, and integrated into, the wider and deeper stretches of the second and third stages of Pip's journey. Born and bred as a gentleman and destined to find happiness and congenial employment through the efforts of others, his function as Pip's *alter ego* is an obvious one. But, like Biddy, he has to stay in the story until the moral plot has been satisfactorily worked out—and Pip has emerged from his dream world—and so, for the present-day reader, he shares in some of the sentimental atmosphere with which Dickens invests the last chapters of the novel. His very last speech in the novel (Chapter 55) gives a clear example of Dickens's power of realising a character's development by means of dialogue:

'And then I shall come back for the dear little thing, and the dear little thing and I will walk quietly into the nearest church. Remember! The blessed darling comes of no family, my dear Handel, and never looked into the red book, and hasn't a notion about her grandpapa. What a fortune for the son of my mother!' (After this moment of critical self-awareness the reference to Herbert at the end of Chapter 58 is quite superfluous, unless it serves to demonstrate Pip's need to tidy up his narrative before the final curtain falls.) Joe, too, has to undergo many chameleon-like changes of character because his original, grotesquely conceived part in the story is affected by the novelist's deepening purpose once the second Stage of Pip's progress is under way. The symbolic function of his character is writ large: like Biddy (and Orlick) he stands for an older, virtuous (or evil) way of life untouched by a society which bases its standards on the possession of unearned wealth. Like them, too, he is conceived in terms of an older stage-convention in which Mr. Wopsle would have felt quite at home. But, under the softening and educative influence of Biddy the gratuitous comic touches —traces of the rather foolish, too good-natured, giant—are erased from his character until only the occasional reversion to dialect and the phrase 'dear old chap' remain. Significantly, too, when Pip has to meet the murderous challenge of Orlick's hatred—a theme that runs right back to the story's beginning—Joe is absent from the marsh-land: Pip has to meet this crisis on his own, unsustained by the antique virtues for which Joe stands, like Adam in *As You Like It*. There is no subtlety in his portrait; his actions never surprise us, not are we sceptical of other people's widely differing reactions to him. His character lives through his speeches which—like those of some Ben Jonson or Sheridan character —are sympathetically conceived. The dialect he speaks is, of course, a stage dialect; we accept its 'genuineness' because we know in our hearts (not in our minds) the special virtues that Joe represents and with which momentarily we are ready to identify ourselves.

The characters of Miss Havisham, and Mr. Jaggers are more complex than this because reader, author and narrator are so entangled in their presentation. On the surface Miss Havisham belongs as much to the world of childhood fable as does Joe or Biddy or Orlick: in the early days of Pip's first Stage she evokes memories of the Snow Maiden and the Witch of Teutonic fairy-tales. For, at this period in his recollections, Pip himself tends to think of various incidents in terms of boyhood fables. When he sets out for London and takes his leave of Miss Havisham (Chapter 19) this childhood vision of his early life is still dominant:

'She looked at Sarah Pocket with triumph in her weird eyes, and so I left my fairy godmother, with both her hands on her crutch stick, standing in the midst of the dimly lighted room beside the rotten bride-cake that was hidden in cobwebs.'

Thereafter Miss Havisham is involved more deeply in the social implications of the moral fable; later still, she is intricately entangled in the recapitulated earlier history of Magwitch, Compeyson and Arthur. Throughout the second Stage of Pip's career she, too, participates in this desperate game of educating a young adolescent for the adult, social world. As this process draws to its close (Chapter 38), in one of the usual set stage-pieces of dialogue which Dickens adopts in order to develop

c

the Estella–Miss Havisham relationship, the fairy godmother discovers that her system of unsentimental education has a cutting side to it. Estella, she finds, can be 'hard and proud' to her benefactress as well as to the rest of mankind. From this moment Dickens alters Miss Havisham's character, while retaining the bizarre setting in which she was initially conceived. During the third Stage the reader not only becomes possessed of all the facts of her pre-history, he is made to feel sympathy and compassion for her desperate attempts to redress ancient wrongs and to cross the boundaries that separate her nightmare world from the common daylight of normal existence.

At first Jaggers emerges from the shadowy background of Satis House as an odd figure with a typical Dickensian gesture by which he can be recognised. He swiftly dominates the second Stage of the novel and, in time, spills over into the novel's pre-history. And yet his character never takes on its own independent life, as Joe's character seems to do whenever Dickens begins to invent dialogue for him to say. In a note on the genesis of *Chance* Conrad writes in these terms about the principal character: 'I simply followed Captain Anthony. Each of us was bent on capturing his own dream.' Jaggers certainly grows in significance as the story progresses. The more we learn about him and his methods the deeper becomes our involvement in the conflict between natural justice and legal administration, and, for added measure, the clearer becomes our understanding of Dickens's constant reference to his accusing finger and his perpetual, Pilate-like washing of his hands. He becomes the receptacle for Dickens's intense feelings about the problem of crime and punishment and the means whereby the author can draw upon his fascinated visual memories of courts, prisons and the underworld. Nor does Dickens miss the opportunity to use this superb performer as the principal character in a series of powerful dramatic scenes. And yet the full potential of this character is never realised within the pages of the novel. Apart from a few touches Jaggers remains a public figure acting out his life in a public capacity: even the motivation of his long domination of Molly is never made explicit from the narrative or expressed in clear terms by either Pip or his creator. In the last resort we realise that Dickens does not rely on character analysis, but on appropriate dialogue and contrived scenes, in order to endow his characters with the verisimilitude of a real existence.

R. W. Stallman (*Forms of Modern Fiction*, p. 234) has elaborately likened the art of fiction to an aquarium and claims that what makes the characters appear as 'life-like' is 'that marvellous liquidity of meaning through which they move'. This is an apt allegory of the kind of life with which Dickens seems to endow Jaggers, Miss Havisham, Joe, Herbert and Biddy once they have been integrated into the rapidly widening world of Pip's second Stage. The remaining characters, Provis and Estella, are so inextricably involved in the central functioning of Pip's recollections and the author's own personal commitment in the situation that he has created, that they cannot be adequately interpreted without the analysis of Pip's dual rôle as actor and narrator of the tale.

3. Pip as Narrator and Protagonist

From the outset Dickens took great care to safeguard *Great Expectations* from the complicated personal involvement which is evident in *David Copperfield* and which, at times, makes the earlier novel such compulsive, magnetic reading. By no stretch of probability can Pip's career be made to run parellel with either that of Dickens or of his forebears. One commentator has made much of Estella's name as a 'lawless anagram' on that of Dickens's mistress, Ellen Lawless Ternan, but even he can make nothing of Magwitch. So successfully has Dickens maintained Pip's fictitious existence that even the moralising comments (or slight touches of a 'layman's religion'), which are present in many of his contributions to *Household Words* and *All The Year Around*, occur infrequently in the course of the novel. Pip believes to some extent in supernatural hints of coming events and he is very sensitive to the promptings of a guilty conscience, but these qualities are consistently portrayed as part of his nature. Similarly, the boy who was only partially cowed by his sister's crude principles of right and wrong and who broke so many rules in order to help the convict on the marsh is still recognisably the young man who decided to seek rough justice for Provis and who refused to believe that the full panoply of English Law had the right to condemn him to death. The warmth of his affections and his basic impulsiveness are clearly portrayed in everything that he does. His devotion to Estella and to Herbert, like his ardent pursuit of the ideal of gentlemanly conduct, form but one side of a coin that matches his other less noble actions: the fierce rejection of Joe in the second Stage, the undisguised repugnance for Provis, the generous self-sacrificing attempt to save Miss Havisham and Magwitch, the visit to the lime-kiln, his instinted admiration for Jaggers's intellect, and even the sudden decision to marry Biddy. Wherever we test it, we find that Pip's character and actions are all of a piece: the character is finely conceived and carefully portrayed with considerable psychological verisimilitude.

There are many moments in the story when the reader dislikes Pip but such moments lie rarely, if ever, outside the novelist's control. Pip is himself his own severe critic and on the whole Dickens has succeeded in saving him from smugness or hypocrisy. Many examples of such critical moments in the reader-narrator relationship could be brought forward, but the best proof of Dickens's success in maintaining this particular knife-edge balance rests on our acceptance of the authenticity of the entire narrative, from the enlarged over-size world of the young Pip's memories of the graveyard to the careful understatement of the final chapter.

Our acceptance of the apparent verisimilitude of the narrative depends largely upon Dickens's skill in the gradual unfolding and matching of events so that each revelation, when it occurs, latches on to existing information that the reader already possesses. The validity of Dickens's employment of repeated symbols, scenes and incidents depends on our acceptance of Pip's veracity as an observer which, in its turn, guarantees the unity of conception of the entire narrative as an exploration through memory of significant, causally-related events that occurred the day before yesterday. The careful plotting which marks this tightly con-structed narrative creates a suitable, external form for the content of the tale which is based upon, and closely follows, a middle-aged man's probings into the formative years of his life. As the narrative progresses forward in time, the interrelatedness of events and principal characters is extended backwards into the novel's pre-history, until all the relevant facts are laid bare and a clear-eyed but chastened Pip is linked to a sub-dued and softened Estella at a place which is close to the story's origins.

This circular plot-movement is closely paralleled by Pip's relationships with two other principal characters, Magwitch and Estella. Magwitch's picaro nature and false notions of gentility are reflected in Pip's own life; each shows a capacity for sustained and self-sacrificing devotion to another person and, at the end of Magwitch's life, Pip seems to mingle his passion for Estella with his frenetic devotion to her father. The grotesque tragi-comic conception with which Dickens began the story is never completely abandoned, for, although it is difficult to swallow within the context of the novel, the reader is expected to accept Estella as the child of Magwitch and Molly. The more one reflects on this relationship (and the final assumption that Estella marries Pip, the narrator) the more difficult it becomes to accept Pip's story as essentially a clearly-defined attack on a whole society and the more powerful do the picaresque and fairy-tale aspects of the story appear to be. For the purposes of the tale Magwitch, Estella and Pip are rootless in origins, unlocated in society and free from obligations to the ordinary claims of the average citizen. The relationship of Magwitch and Estella to other characters in the story is predatory and (in their different ways) destructive; the positive aspects of their nature are preserved only in Pip's memory of their conversations and acts with him. Even the final meeting between Pip and Estella is occasioned by their joint acts of memory, 'realised' in a place, rather than by any willed desire to find each other and so establish a new fruitful relationship. In Pip's eyes all three of them have expiated their past crimes independently and when he and Estella leave the ruined garden a chapter in their lives has been irrevocably and finally closed. *whether they are to us is left open.*

Conceived as outsiders, Magwitch and Estella still react violently against the other characters and against the ordinary conventions of 'society', in so far as that term can be used for the loosely-connected locations in which Pip's story is enacted. Magwitch is classless, almost codeless, and a creature of instinctive obsessions; he has all the marks of a frontiersman who is at home only in the open air. Australia, with its wide spaces (and its solitude), is the ideal place for him to make a fortune. And yet he is impelled to return to, and to clash with, an older society which has rejected him from childhood. He is the touchstone by which all the false notions of gentility and breeding are tested and found wanting and, ultimately, his devotion to Pip's memory—the sole positive virtue in his make-up—brings about Pip's own regeneration. Magwitch's narrative of his life's story is one of Dickens's supreme strokes of artistry: it pulls together many hidden threads of narrative and, at the same time, acts as a testimony in justification of his conduct. Thereafter Magwitch's biography dominates the novel's social content like a jagged rocky outcrop above fields of corn: the eye is forcibly drawn back to it in wonder and enquiry. Estella, too, possesses the same catalytic quality. Apart from her rôle as Pip's adored one—the one spark of self-effacement in his middle stage of development—her principal function in the novel is to pour doubt on the excessive feelings of those who surround her and to stand for those principles of passionless reason (based on self-interest and twisted ideals) which, Dickens seems to suggest, lie at the heart of a genteel, acquisitive society. She operates in the private world of the affections while her father's conduct provokes conflict with the public claims of society. Conceived in obscurity, concealed as an infant, educated in the twilight world of Satis House and brought to maturity in the social night life of the fashionable world, she is gentle only with

Pip (travelling on the open road) and expresses her own sense of inadequate development (in Chapter 38) as part of her inability 'to take naturally to the daylight'. Like Miss Havisham, Estella seems to lack an independent existence of her own, until disaster claims her and bitter experience softens her nature. For Dickens's powerful, grotesque portrait of Satis House and its inhabitants has been too successfully executed. Despite the admirable exchanges of dialogue there between Pip, Miss Havisham, Jaggers and Estella, those sections of the novel that are located within its walls remain stage scenes redolent of melodrama and pantomime. Even Estella's one firm link with society—her marriage to Drummle—is tinged with farce because he is no more than a flat, pasteboard character: there are countless characters like him in Restoration and eighteenth-century comedy, with a label, 'Upper-Class Booby', around his neck and with no independent realisation in terms of action or dialogue. Unlike Magwitch, Estella is never completely integrated into the social theme which Dickens developed out of and around the Never-Never Land of Pip's first Stage of life.

Both Estella and her father are indissolubly linked with Pip's own recollected life: they draw much of their vitality directly from his peculiarly personal vision of, and judgement upon, the kind of life they have been compelled to live by the pressure of external circumstances. Pip's desperate, self-punishing search for Estella's true antecedents is presented to the reader in stronger terms and with more cogency than the effect of that discovery upon the future course of events can warrant. The discovery does not help Magwitch—even his recognition of the fact is uncertain; the status of Molly is never raised once the answer has been found, and Estella is never informed of the fact. Why is this? What purpose does this particular line of enquiry serve in the carefully formulated construction of the novel? Possibly, this search for Estella's ancestry could be interpreted as an unconscious blunder on Dickens's part. He sedulously shielded his children and his friends from any knowledge of the black (ungenteel?) spots in his own education and childhood training. There is some mystification in the close parallels that exist between parts of *David Copperfield* and his own unpublished autobiographical fragment. He has left on record a bitter denunciation of his parent's neglect of his formal education. Are we not justified in assuming that, because *Great Expectations* is shaped from some of the more sensitive spots in Dickens's own childhood memories, he would at times be unable to control his pen and would explore imaginatively certain suppressed areas of his own life, even if such exploration was irrelevant to Pip's story? I think this is a mistaken view of the novel. Naturally, Dickens drew on his own childhood recollections for much of the detail of Pip's childhood, grotesque though it is, and, to this extent, Pip sees and hears the world through Dickens's own senses. But Pip cannot be confused with Dickens and Dickens has taken great pains to keep their identities apart. The carefully interwoven plot construction, the repeated themes, symbols and images, the studied care taken over details of time and place, all show Dickens's determination to 'distance' Pip's narrative and so to separate Pip's life story from his own. The author of *Great Expectations* was a wealthy man, assured of his place in society, with distinct and vocal opinions on social and moral questions and, above all, with a shrewd capacity for exploiting an acquisitive society for his own profit. Pip's ineptitude is made acceptable to us, not because of his failure to achieve great material expectations, but because we are made to share his search for personal identity. His tortured self-questionings and periodic moments of severe self-examination are part of his nature; we quickly learn to accept them as his own without attributing them to the author. They are no more out of place here than are those of Christian in *Pilgrim's Progress*, and for the same reason: they objectify preoccupations shared at some time by all human beings. Pip's ultimate standards of moral judgement are vitiated by the intellectual weakness of theological debate in Victorian England, but nothing can dim one's admiration for his single-minded pursuit of the truth as he sees it. The search for Estella's identity forms part of this pursuit and is complementary to the constant enquiry into the springs of his own conduct throughout all the actions that follow upon that first casual encounter in the graveyard. As Pip ponders the life story of Magwitch and Estella, in order to shape his narrative, he finds reasons and excuses for *their* conduct too; and, as the narrative grows, all the other characters are subjected to the same critical scrutiny. In the process the functions of the acceptable social code, of the rule of law, of the claims of religion, of education, of the family, and of the sources of wealth are involved in Pip's obstinate questionings and are subordinated to his ultimate demand for personal fulfilment through the provision of opportunities for acceptable employment (outside England) and domestic happiness. 'The bitterness of Dickens's exposure of Pip's parasitism' (G. B. Shaw) is followed by a modified happiness which is based on a reconciliation to the claims of society and of other individuals upon him.

A. O. J. Cockshut detects a faltering in the 'devastating satirical demands' of the story and suggests that *Great Expectations* reveals 'a new timidity' in Dickens's critique of Victorian England. Such a conclusion ignores the novelist's careful attempts to keep the narrative within the fallible bounds of Pip's memory which, in the event, attracts to itself those incidents and events that are most deeply involved with Pip's own personal history. As the threads of the narrative are pulled together the reader senses some of that artificial telescoping of events which is common to most of Dickens's novels, except that in *Great Expectations* this matters less and arouses fewer question marks than the end of *David Copperfield*. The novel turns naturally and inevitably upon itself and we are left to assume that the orphan child, who began his tale with a backward look and some uncertainty about his own name, has at last found a companion and some modified assurance upon which to build his future expectations. The fairy-tale that developed into an allegory has at last become an ordinary, human pilgrimage.

4. *Style*

During the last two decades interpreters of Dickens's novels have paid an inordinate amount of attention to the social implications of his novels, to their relationship to Victorian society and to the symbols and themes that lie hidden like reefs just beneath the surface of his rapidly moving narrative. As a result of this concentration of interest on the sociological and, indeed, psychological implications of his novels—particularly the later ones—less close attention has been given to the quality of Dickens's style. For this reason alone this chapter will contain typical examples of the many different kinds of writing in this one novel in order to suggest that the chameleon-like quality of Dickens's style in *Great Expectations* is part of the novel's strength, and, at the same time, contains clear evidence of the novel's weaknesses. In *David Copperfield* there is a great deal of compulsive writing: one feels that the narrator is pouring out his heart and for long stretches of the novel one is unable to put it down, so intense is the urgency of the narrator's tone. *Great Expectations* is written in a much more 'distanced' manner: Dickens allows Pip to relate incidents and events which are similar to sensitive spots in the novelist's own life without becoming too deeply involved himself in the narration. Mr. T. S. Eliot's dictum, that 'the more perfect the artist, the more completely separate in him will be the man who suffers and the mind which creates', expresses succinctly my considered opinion of Dickens's aim—if not his final achievement—in this second attempt at an imaginative re-creation of the 'twice told tales of infancy'.

George Orwell's opinion that Dickens's fertility of invention consists 'not so much of characters and situations, as of turns of phrase and concrete details' is echoed by most critics. Shaw learned from Dickens 'that it is possible to combine a mirror-like exactness of character drawing with the wildest extravagances of humorous expression'; H. Blair Rouse praises Dickens because he adapted his reporter's gifts to express a 'sense of history in physical action and surface portrayals'; John H. Hagan believes that in order to give his theme 'imaginative embodiment' Dickens is constantly bringing concrete images from the marsh-land, the mud and the hulks into the apparently tranquil indoor life of the novel.

At all times Dickens is in control of his gift for intense visual recall. The following passage (from Chapter 40) shows his ability to use the observation of details in order to convey Pip's shrinking from Provis:

'The influences of his solitary hut-life were upon him besides, and gave him a savage air that no dress could tame; added to these were the influences of his subsequent branded life among men, and crowning all, his consciousness that he was dodging and hiding now. In all his ways of sitting and standing, and eating and drinking—of brooding about, in a high-shouldered reluctant style—of taking out his great horn-handled jackknife and wiping it on his legs and cutting his food—of lifting light glasses and cups to his lips, as if they were clumsy pannikins—of chopping a wedge off his bread, and soaking up with it the last fragments of gravy round and round his plate, as if to make the most of an allowance, and then drying his fingers on it, and then swallowing it—in these ways and in a thousand other small nameless instances arising every minute in the day, there was Prisoner, Felon, Bondsman, plain as plain could be.'

In contrast to these staccato phrases the following rhetorical account of Pip's delirium (Chapter 57) seems to convey the wandering movement of the patient:

'That I had a fever and was avoided, that I suffered greatly, that I often lost my reason, that the time seemed interminable, that I confounded impossible existences with my own identity; that I was a brick in the house wall, and yet entreating to be released from the giddy place where the builders had set me; that I was a steel beam of a vast engine, clashing and whirling over a gulf, and yet that I implored in my own person to have the engine stopped, and my part in it hammered off; that I passed through these phases of disease, I know of my own remembrance, and did in some sort know at the time. That I sometimes struggled with real people, in the belief that they were murderers, and that I would all at once comprehend that they meant to do me good, and would then sink exhausted in their arms, and suffer them to lay me down, I also knew at the time. But, above all, I knew that there was a constant tendency in all these people—who, when I was very ill, would present all kinds of extraordinary transformations of the human face, and would be much dilated in size—above all, I say, I knew that there was an extraordinary tendency in all these people, sooner or later, to settle down into the likeness of Joe.'

Great Expectations was carefully designed in three emergent stages that
assist the reader to share Pip's ever-deepening probes into the suppressed
layers of recollection. The simplicity of the relation of childhood
memories in Stage One is reflected in a general directness of style: the
texture of Stage Three is much more complex, for, as the action speeds
up, it is accompanied by substantial revelations about the pre-history of
Magwitch, Compeyson, Miss Havisham and Estella, which are reflected
in more frequent echoes of images and scenes from the two earlier
stages. Graham Greene believes that this novel was written in 'delicate
and exact poetic cadences, the music of memory, that so influenced
Proust'. The two extracts that follow (the first from Chapter 48 and
the second from Chapter 58) show the consistency with which Dickens
used this device of recall in order to create two quite distinct moods:

'He dismissed her, and she glided out of the room. But she remained
before me, as plainly as if she were still there. I looked at those hands,
I looked at those eyes, I looked at that flowing hair; and I compared
them with other hands, other eyes, other hair, that I knew of, and with
what those might be after twenty years of a brutal husband and a stormy
life. I looked again at those hands and eyes of the housekeeper, and
thought of the inexplicable feeling that had come over me when I last
walked—not alone—in the ruined garden, and through the deserted
brewery. I thought how the same feeling had come back when I saw
a face looking at me, and a hand waving to me, from a stage-coach
window; and how it had come back again and had flashed about me like
lightning, when I had passed in a carriage—not alone—through a sudden
glare of light in a dark street. I thought how one link of association had
helped that identification in the theatre, and how such a link, wanting
before, had been riveted for me now, when I had passed by a chance
swift from Estella's name to the fingers with their knitting action, and
the attentive eyes. And I felt absolutely certain that this woman was
Estella's mother.'

'The June weather was delicious. The sky was blue, the larks were
soaring high over the green corn, I thought all that country-side more
beautiful and peaceful by far than I had ever known it to be yet. Many
pleasant pictures of the life that I would lead there, and of the change for
the better that would come over my character when I had a guiding
spirit at my side whose simple faith and clear home-wisdom I had

proved, beguiled my way. They awakened a tender emotion in me; for my heart was softened by my return, and such a change had come to pass, that I felt like one who was toiling home barefoot from distant travel, and whose wanderings had lasted many years.

'The schoolhouse where Biddy was mistress, I had never seen; but the little roundabout lane, by which I entered the village for quietness' sake, took me past it. I was disappointed to find that the day was a holiday; no children were there, and Biddy's house was closed. Some hopeful notion of seeing her, busily engaged in her daily duties, before she saw me, had been in my mind and was defeated.

'But the forge was a very short distance off, and I went towards it under the sweet green limes, listening for the clink of Joe's hammer. Long after I ought to have heard it, and long after I had fancied I heard it and found it but a fancy, all was still. The limes were there, and the white thorns were there, and the chestnut-trees were there, and their leaves rustled harmoniously when I stopped to listen; but the clink of Joe's hammer was not in the midsummer wind.

'Almost fearing, without knowing why, to come in view of the forge, I saw it at last, and saw it was closed. No gleam of fire, no glittering shower of sparks, no roar of bellows; all shut up, and still.'

The kinds of narrative prose given above form a considerable part of the staple style of the novel; but, although Dickens takes considerable pains to remind the reader that it is Pip's eye that has seen these things, Pip's memory that recalls them, and Pip's voice that gives them expression, he also relies heavily on reported dialogue in order to support Pip's memories with the suggestion that it depends scrupulously on fact. Walter C. Phillips (*Dickens, Reade, and Collins, Sensation Novelists*, p. 219) has argued that *Great Expectations*, like the work of Reade and Collins, is a significant milestone in the progress from the long, discursive three-decker novel to the later one-volume story: there was among these novelists (grouped around Dickens) a pronounced taste for villainy, violence, and crime, but they adopted a refinement of method which included a 'mode of expression that is necessary for a play'. They liked to call their works dramatic novels. Dickens had always relied on invented, fantastic dialogue as a foil to his vividly reported, descriptive scenes; in his mature novels he came to rely heavily on the use of appropriate dialogue. *Great Expectations* is rich in illustrations of his gift for reported speech that is at once 'realistic' and dramatic. Miss Havisham would never have left her fairy-tale attic but for her later verbal exchanges with Estella and Pip; Jaggers lives for us largely through his words; Joe's own fantastic brand of English endears him to us much more than the incidents which describe him as the soft-hearted giant. Chapter 22, with the long conversation between Pip and Herbert about the latter's expectations, is a good example of Dickens's ability to adapt ordinary conversation to the advancement of his story and to our knowledge of its characters. The long undulating exchange between Jaggers and Pip in Chapter 40 (about Provis—'in New South Wales') shows Dickens's constant determination, and ability, to relieve moments of tension in the plot by a series of theatrical interchanges. (Is this fixed determination of the novelist to enliven the more sombre parts of Pip's memories the reason for A. O. J. Cockshut's opinion that, because the theme is 'deadly serious', the 'tone is too jolly'?) There is always, of course, the danger that the novelist's dialogue becomes too literary for all dramatic purposes: a danger that is always present in the later stages of the novel when Estella is the object of memory. This passage, for example, from Chapter 44 can belong only to the author, who quickly makes Pip call it a 'rhapsody':

' "Out of my thoughts! You are part of my existence, part of myself. You have been in every line I have ever read, since I first came here, the rough common boy whose poor heart you wounded even then. You have been in every prospect I have ever seen since—on the river, on the sails of the ships, on the marshes, in the clouds, in the light, in the darkness, in the wind, in the woods, in the sea, in the streets. You have been the embodiment of every graceful fancy that my mind has ever become acquainted with. The stones of which the strongest London buildings are made, are not more real, or more impossible to be displaced by your hands, than your presence and influence have been to me, there and everywhere, and will be. Estella, to the last hour of my life, you cannot choose but remain part of my character, part of the little good in me, part of the evil. But, in this separation I associate you only with the good, and I will faithfully hold you to that always, for you must have done me far more good than harm, let me feel now what sharp distress I may. O God bless you, God forgive you!" '

As Pip's rhapsody suggests, the oft-repeated charge against Dickens's sentimentalism can be brought against some of the writing in *Great Expectations*. Generally such passages jar on the modern reader and, after every allowance has been made for Victorian taste, one regrets that Dickens wrote them. A defence of some of them could be made because the novel is itself an account of a 'sentimental education' that leads to Pip's greater self-awareness; however, it is well to note, first, that the moments of sentimentalism are clustered around certain characters only and, secondly, that Dickens was capable of breaking the sentimental mood at will. Estella, naturally, attracts to herself all Pip's desire to dwell longingly over the past. The following extract (from Chapter 33) illustrates admirably how a passage that begins with firmness of tone can suddenly degenerate into sentimental observation:

'We came to Richmond all too soon, and our destination there was a house by the Green: a staid old house, where hoops and powder and patches, embroidered coats, rolled stockings, ruffles, and swords, had had their court days many a time. Some ancient trees before the house were still cut into fashions as formal and unnatural as the hoops and wigs and stiff skirts; but their own allotted places in the great procession of the dead were not far off, and they would soon drop into them and go the silent way of the rest.

'A bell with an old voice—which I dare say in its time had often said to the house, Here is the green farthingale, Here is the diamond-hilted sword, Here are the shoes with red heels and the blue solitaire,—sounded gravely in the moonlight, and two cherry-coloured maids came fluttering out to receive Estella. The doorway soon absorbed her boxes, and she gave me her hand and a smile, and said good night, and was absorbed likewise. And still I stood looking at the house, thinking how happy I should be if I lived there with her, and knowing that I never was happy with her, but always miserable.

'I got into the carriage to be taken back to Hammersmith, and I got in with a bad heart-ache, and I got out with a worse heart-ache. At our own door I found little Jane Pocket coming home from a little party, escorted by her little lover; and I envied her little lover, in spite of his being subject to Flopson.'

Dickens has a much firmer grip on Pip's betrayal of his feelings for Joe. (Biddy is quite a different proposition!) Chapter 57 provides many examples of Dickens's power to walk the knife-edge between sentimental gush and the conveying of tenderness in human relationships. Joe's special brand of humorous dialogue, however stagey in origin, is the means by which Dickens contrives to keep his balance:

'For the tenderness of Joe was so beautifully proportioned to my need, that I was like a child in his hands. He would sit and talk to me in the old confidence, and with the old simplicity, and in the old un-assertive protecting way, so that I would half believe that all my life since the days of the old kitchen was one of the mental troubles of the fever that was gone. He did everything for me except the household work, for which he had engaged a very decent woman, after paying off the laundress on his first arrival. " Which I do assure you, Pip," he would often say, in explanation of that liberty; "I found her a tapping the spare bed, like a cask of beer, and drawing off the feathers in a bucket, for sale. Which she would have tapped yourn next, and draw'd it off with you a laying on it, and was then a carrying away the coals gradiw-ally in the soup-tureen and wegetable dishes, and the wine and spirits in your Wellington boots." '

A similar dexterity in the use of verbal humour (and grotesque visual-isation) as a secure bridge across the cosy domestic tears of much Victor-ian literature is shown superbly in the description of Mrs. Joe's funeral (in Chapter 35). Sentiment and *pietas* is never outraged, but the phoney quality of the set funeral is acidly and humorously summed up in Mr. Trabb's businesslike injunction—' "Pocket-handkerchiefs out! We are ready!" ' There can be no ready-made charge of sentimentalism against Dickens when such passages are read carefully. Conrad's preface to *The Nigger of the Narcissus*—a similar act of fictional exploration of autobiographical memories is, perhaps, a safe guide to this problem of how to give due place to the emotions in a novel:—'The changing wisdom of successive generations discards ideas, questions, facts, demolishes theories. But the artist appeals to that part of our being which is not dependent on wisdom; to that in us which is a gift and not an acquisition—and, therefore, more permanently enduring. He speaks to our capacity for delight and wonder, to the sense of mystery surround-ing our lives; to our sense of pity, and beauty, and pain; to the latent feeling of fellowship with all creation—and to the subtle but invincible conviction of solidarity that knits together the loneliness of innumerable hearts, to the solidarity in dreams, in joy, in sorrow, in aspirations, in illusions, in hope, in fear, which binds men to each other, which binds together all humanity—the dead to the living and the living to the unborn.'

If the question of Dickens's sentimentality is a thorny one, the discussion of his humour is a thicket, almost impenetrable to contemporary critics, particularly in analyses of his later works. Dickens was not wedded indissolubly to his comic Muse. Professors Butt and Tillotson (*Dickens at Work*, p. 22) have noted that when Dickens had written too much for any serial number he 'was accustomed to make his cuts at the expense of the comedy'. Dickens, one must assume on the evidence of his periodical writing, never lost the gift for comic invention of dialogue or for the grotesque embroidery and exaggeration of incidents encountered in his constant journeyings and restless walks. I agree with Edgar Johnson (*Charles Dickens: His Tragedy and Triumph*, p. 993) that *Great Expectations* is 'not a melancholy book' in its pervading atmosphere and that 'these joyous moments do not undermine the predominant serious-ness . . . of its theme'. Since it is part of the author's intention that Pip's narrative should catch up within itself half a lifetime's recollections, the novel must of necessity contain many kinds of humour. The exagger-ated, over-serious childhood memories of the adult world, the vividly etched adolescent memories of Satis House, the uncomfortable and irritating memories of Trabb's boy, the patronisingly recalled stages in Mr. Wopsle's histrionic decline and fall, the benevolence that surrounds all the oddities of Wemmick's fantastic life, and the affectionate yet whimsical portrayal of Herbert as a boy, a young man and a business-man—these are staple elements in the texture of Pip's mind as well as in the unfolding events of his life. Other incidents are clearly brought for-ward by the author for our extraneous enjoyment: the young men at Finches Grove, Mrs. Joe on the Rampage, Pumblechook at all times, Mr. and Mrs. Matthew Pocket at home, and Pip and Drummle before the inn fire, are some examples of Dickens's fine sense of the entertain-ment expected of Boz by the reading public.

The comic style is varied and it can become mannered and fall into a reliance on verbal tricks:

'And here I may remark that when Mr. Wopsle referred to me, he considered it a necessary part of such reference to rumple my hair and poke it into my eyes. I cannot conceive why everybody of his standing who visited at our house should always have put me through the same inflammatory process under similar circumstances. Yet I do not call to mind that I was ever in my earlier youth the subject of remark in our social family circle, but some large-handed person took some such ophthalmic steps to patronise me' (Chapter 10).

D

Such a drop in the tension of the writing is frequent in the first stage of Pip's tale and is never quite absent from the entire treatment of Wemmick. Even so, the facetiousness of the following account of his marriage (Chapter 55) is so rare in the third Stage that one suspects Dickens of a desire to send Wemmick out of the story with a boisterous slap of warm-hearted gratitude:

' "Halloa!" said Wemmick. "Here's Miss Skiffins! Let's have a wedding."

'That discreet damsel was attired as usual, except that she was now engaged in substituting for her green kid gloves, a pair of white. The Aged was likewise occupied in preparing a similar sacrifice for the altar of Hymen. The old gentleman, however, experienced so much difficulty in getting his gloves on, that Wemmick found it necessary to put him with his back against a pillar, and then to get behind the pillar himself and pull away at them, while I for my part held the old gentleman round the waist, that he might present an equal and safe resistance. By dint of this ingenious scheme, his gloves were got on to perfection.

'The clerk and clergyman then appearing, we were ranged in order at those fatal rails. True to his notion of seeming to do it all without preparation, I heard Wemmick say to himself as he took something out of his waistcoat-pocket before the service began, "Halloa! Here's a ring!" '

To discount the author's insistence on retaining this tone of good-humoured recollection and to concentrate one's critical attention too closely on the interwoven memories of mist, marsh-land, dark water, mud and prison stench could lead the reader to a lop-sided understanding of Pip's own character and philosophy of life.

Naturally a novel of this length has its passages of tired writing. The indeterminate movement of the following passage (Chapter 16)—quite typical of many of Pip's attempts to come to terms with his sense of guilt—cannot be blamed entirely upon the tone of Lillo's *George Barnwell*:

'It was horrible to think that I had provided the weapon, however undesignedly, but I could hardly think otherwise. I suffered unspeakable trouble while I considered and reconsidered whether I should at last dissolve that spell of my childhood and tell Joe all the story. For months afterwards, I every day settled the question finally in the negative, and reopened and reargued it next morning. The contention came, after all, to this;—the secret was such an old one now, had so grown into me and become a part of myself, that I could not tear it away. In addition to the dread that, having led up to so much mischief, it would be now more likely than ever to alienate Joe from me if he believed it, I had a further restraining dread that he would not believe it, but would assert it with the fabulous dogs and veal-cutlets as a monstrous invention. However, I temporised with myself, of course—for was I not wavering between right and wrong, when the thing is always done?—and resolved to make a full disclosure if I should see any such new occasion as a new chance of helping in the discovery of the assailant.' (A similar inability to give satisfactory expression to the vague promptings of the subconscious mind can be found at the end of Chapter 32.)

At times, too, Dickens's strongly developed visual sense comes between him and the reader. He overdoes the sensational aspect of Orlick's attempt on Pip's life or the fantastic upstairs life of Bill Barley without adding to the pace of the narrative or to our understanding of these minor characters. On the whole Chapter 54 is an exciting and remarkably consistent piece of writing, but even here the visual details can get in the way and, as a consequence, the style flags:

'Our oarsmen were so fresh, by dint of having occasionally let her drive with the tide for a minute or two, that a quarter of an hour's rest proved full as much as they wanted. We got ashore among some slippery stones while we ate and drank what we had with us, and looked about. It was like my own marsh country, flat and monotonous, and with a dim horizon; while the winding river turned and turned, and the great floating buoys upon it turned and turned, and everything else seemed stranded and still. For now the last of the fleet of ships was round the last low point we had headed; and the last green barge, straw-laden, with a brown sail, had followed; and some ballast-lighters, shaped like a child's first rude imitation of a boat, lay low in the mud; and a little squat shoal-lighthouse on open piles, stood crippled in the mud on stilts and crutches; and slimy stakes stuck out of the mud, and slimy stones stuck out of the mud, and red landmarks and tidemarks stuck out of the mud, and an old landing-stage and an old roofless building slipped into the mud, and all about us was stagnation and mud.'

The most notorious example of Dickens's 'set-piece style' is the frequently quoted end of Chapter 38:

'And now that I have given the one chapter to the theme that so filled my heart, and so often made it ache and ache again, I pass on, unhindered, to the event that had impended over me longer yet; the event that had begun to be prepared for, before I knew that the world held Estella, and in the days when her baby intelligence was receiving its first distortions from Miss Havisham's wasting hands.

'In the Eastern story, the heavy slab that was to fall on the bed of state in the flush of conquest was slowly wrought out of the quarry, the tunnel for the rope to hold it in its place was slowly carried through the leagues of rock, the slab was slowly raised and fitted in the roof, the rope was rove to it and slowly taken through the miles of hollow to the great iron ring. All being made ready with much labour, and the hour come, the sultan was aroused in the dead of the night, and the sharpened axe that was to sever the rope from the great iron ring was put into his hand, and he struck with it, and the rope parted and rushed away, and the ceiling fell. So in my case; all the work, near and afar, that tended to the end, had been accomplished; and in an instant the blow was struck, and the roof of my stronghold dropped upon me.'

The tone even of this passage, with its air of apparent detachment and its obvious direct address to the reader, is a rare one in the novel. For it is rather wild to discuss the 'style' of *Great Expectations* as one would discuss the style of Conrad or James Joyce. Apart from the more obvious characteristics of Dickens's gifts as a writer—his eye for significant detail, his ear for comic utterance, his assured command of all the oratorical tricks directed at a known audience—there is a sense in which, in his novels, Dickens had no recognisable 'style' at all. (His periodical style of writing is much more uniform in texture, tone and cadence.) He possessed in abundance a vital energy which enabled him to carry his story forward and the reader with it. Some of his worst excesses derive from his acute awareness of the waiting audience; his excellences, too, depend upon his determination to satisfy that audience's demand for a story. His superb self-assurance does the rest.

5. Themes and Symbols

Recent critics like Edmund Wilson, Lionel Trilling, Edgar Johnson, David Daiches, Monroe Engel, John H. Hagan, John H. Raleigh, Graham Greene and A. O. J. Cockshut have helped to uncover many of the themes and symbols that are embodied in the narrative of Pip's quest for self-fulfilment. To write down a catalogue of all the themes that emerge, in moments of reflection after successive readings of the novel, is to create scepticism about a pre-emptive claim for any single theme as the sole key to the labyrinth of the story's meaning. The list seems endless: crime and punishment; natural justice and the law; pre-destination and free will; the outcast and society; the dignity of labour in an acquisitive society; private lives and public pretensions; the relationship between the instincts and the affections; the operation of time in events and in the subconscious mind; the idea of consequences from one generation to the next; the rôle of education in one's progress towards clear self-awareness; private belief and public profession; the sharp juxtaposition of appearance and reality; violence as a counterpart of 'gentility'. This is by no means an exhaustive list of the clear, intellectual concepts that are woven into the tapestry of the narrative and it takes no account of the multiple symbols that Dickens draws upon in the act of writing in order to keep alive the reader's awareness of his themes while the story of Pip's life is being re-enacted before his eyes: the prison hulks and the marsh, the mists of the flat country being incorporated into the shadows of town life, the open-air freedom of the criminals impinging upon the domestic comfort of his families, the frequent use of the four elements at crucial points in the narrative, Estella's plea for daylight as a counterforce to Satis House and all it stands for, the theatricality of church and Courts of Justice, the deserted garden, and the open sea. Once more the list is longer and more overwhelming than any single solution that can be offered as a clue to the novelist's artistic purpose once Dickens had decided to develop his initial 'grotesque tragi-comic conception' along lines that were parallel to, but not contiguous with, the autobiographical success-story of *David Copperfield*. (For Pip, unlike David, decides to recount his life-story when material prosperity and worldly success have escaped him.) The compilation of these catalogues serves a double purpose: it suggests why some writers are tempted to make exaggerated claims for Dickens's universality as though he were a prose Shakespeare, and it focusses the reader's attention on Dickens's ability so to enmesh the selected incidents from his hero's life in the claims of society and the velleities in the operation of the individual will that the ground plot appears to become a moral fable. 'To know a story when we see one, to know it for a story, to know that it is not reality itself but that it has clear and effective relations with reality—this is one of the great disciplines of the mind.' Of course, Lionel Trilling's apotheosis of the ideal novel is not true at all points for *Great Expectations*—chiefly, I suggest, because while Dickens nearly succeeded in identifying himself with Pip, he retained the right to embroider Pip's narrative with direct addresses to his own beloved readers; but it does indicate the kind of success that is achieved in this novel when the reader's imagination is caught and held by the rapid unfolding of the tale.

Dickens's device of a three-part structure has helped him to strip his theme to its intellectual essentials without constricting the free flow of its social and psychological implications. Since the entire artifice is based on Pip's conscious act of memory, and since any act of memory is essentially an exploration of events bounded by causation in time and place, Dickens invests each of the three stages with clear-cut, easily grasped temporal and spatial characteristics. Stage One, acted against the marsh-land, the Forge, the inn, the small town and Satis House, is played out against a clearly defined backcloth at a leisurely pace so that unusual incidents are magnified to occupy a dominant significance in Pip's recall of selected childhood events. Stage Two is set against the metropolitan labyrinth of London—pinpointed for us by excursions away from it—where space is so extensive that time, too, seems limitless. At this stage in their emergence from the chrysalis of formative influences, Pip and Estella are allowed to live carelessly and irresponsibly as though freed from all outside obligations and impelled only by the inner need to find personal fulfilment. Inevitably this illusion of freedom is shattered in Stage Three when the claims of the hidden past reach out and shatter their present dreams (and future actions): the cosy, static world of Stage One and the factitious stage-set interiors of Stage Two are thrown rapidly and disjunctively against public events, natural phenomena, and the open ways of the world on land and sea. The

Thames suddenly becomes the gateway to a wider world; Satis House is destroyed; the Forge becomes a genuine family home; the escaped convict dies at peace in a prison hospital. The reverberations, echoes and chain-reactions of these events are certainly brought to a hurried conclusion as the novel ends, but Dickens's instinct is sound when he shuffles his principal subordinate actors off the stage and quickly leads the reader back to the point of rest (in time and place) where the story began. The final marriage of Pip and Estella (the daughter of Magwitch) is fittingly the central dynamic moment from which the whole act of recollection derives its original impulse.

The novel's end, one may argue, is its true beginning: 'I took her hand in mine, and we went out of the ruined place; and, as the morning mists had risen long ago when I first left the forge, so, the evening mists were rising now, and in all the broad expanse of tranquil light they showed to me, I saw no shadow of another parting from her.' Despite the softening (and sentimentalising?) influence of the mist-image, this sentence, like the rest of this much-disputed, altered ending to *Great Expectations*, is not a betrayal of the story that precedes it. For even in this last chapter the offending mist-image serves many purposes. When Pip enters the ruin 'A cold silvery mist had veiled the afternoon'; when he met Estella and saw 'the saddened softened light of the once proud eyes' and the moon began to rise, Pip was reminded of Magwitch's death ('I thought of the placid look at the white ceiling, which had passed away'.) 'The silvery mist' was then touched for the first time 'with the first rays of moonlight'. The conversation that follows is about practical matters which are still relevant to the theme of *Great Expectations*. At last Estella is selling the ground so that homes can be built on the site of Satis House, while Pip who had been educated to expect an empty, parasitic life of obedience to vague, gentlemanly ideals of good form—those ideals of Matthew Pocket, the Finches or Drummle —confesses, 'I work pretty hard for a sufficient living, and therefore— Yes, I do well!' The restrained and sober confession of love that follows and leads into the mellowed wistfulness of Dickens's last paragraph cannot therefore be interpreted as a weak escape from that sombre indictment of an acquisitive society which has formed the back-bone of the novel's seriousness. That theme is still vibrant as the novel ends. Without a doubt the story displays a restricting contraction of interest once Magwitch has died and Pip falls into delirium, but the story would have been incomplete if Pip's own voyage of self-discovery—couched in terms of a regression to childhood scenes and adolescent fantasies—had not been carried through in terms of narrative and dialogue. Modern taste may recoil from the self-revelatory exchanges between Joe, Biddy and Pip while it accepts gratefully the ironic treatment of Pumblechook, the windy donkey's hypocrisy. (Personally I don't think that Dickens was being 'unrealistic' when he made his characters speak from the heart: my own memory of Victorian great-aunts confirms the accuracy of this reporting of sober country folk with strong Evangelical beliefs.) Pip's narrative would have been incomplete and his need for expiation—the driving force behind his narrative—would have remained unfulfilled if Dickens had not matched the exposure of a false money-centred society with a similar exposure of Pip's and Estella's false sense of values in the conduct of their private lives. The restrained evening glow which suffuses the novel's last sentence has the quality of the final curtain at a theatrical performance: it also reflects a contentment of mind without which, surely, the narrator could never have undertaken his long exploration of the events and attitudes that led him and Estella to this final meeting in the deserted garden which is about to become the centre of re-building and new life. Despite its deflation of all except the most limited and old-fashioned expectations from human existence, the novel is a healing book.

Related though it was to Dickens's domestic problems the analysis of the springs of private happiness is not the novel's dominant concern. Dickens was pleased from the first with the aptness of his title, *Great Expectations*, and Lionel Trilling's interpretation of that approval is basically sound, though slightly exaggerated in emphasis: 'The greatness of *Great Expectations* begins in its title: modern society bases itself on great expectations which, if ever they are realised, are found to exist by reason of a sordid, hidden reality. The real thing is not the gentility of Pip's life but the hulks and the murder and the rats and decay in the cellarage of the novel.' Such a forthright interpretation does insufficient justice to Dickens's artistry, to his continuous attempts to keep telling the story as an act of Pip's mature and mellowed recollection; it removes Joe and Biddy to the margins of the tale and places Magwitch and Compeyson permanently in the central position. The novel has been so skilfully constructed out of a series of interlocking events and thematic convolutions, and the novelist seems to rely so heavily in the later scenes on actual echoes and recalls of earlier events, dialogues and situations, that no simple, unitary solution to its multiple meanings can be found completely acceptable. Monroe Engel has singled out for approval, as a sign of Dickens's increasing, conscious artistry in this novel, the manner in which 'plot, themes, symbols' from the public and private world 'all support each other'. For this reason, perhaps, some critics have expressed a vague dissatisfaction not only with the novel's ending, but also with the ambivalent attitude of Pip towards the events and characters of his story. It is no surprise that a similar ambivalence towards the novel is shown by a variety of critics and this suggests that, apart from certain obvious lessons (about hard work, the need for self-knowledge, and the essential rightness of old-fashioned domestic virtues), the novel raises more questions than it answers. Two major and two minor themes, however, are brought clearly before the reader's conscious mind before the novel ends: parasitism in public and private life is severely condemned, and a large question mark is raised against the operations of human justice; in support of these indictments Dickens constantly reverts to the unfulfilled need for a true form of education that will act as a counterforce not only to the accidents of chance but, more significantly, to the consequences of heredity.

Analysis, based upon successive re-readings of the novel, can show the rigour with which Dickens stripped his theme to a few intellectual conceptions, but the reader still remembers that these basic ideas are surrounded by thousands of observed pieces of detail, innumerable remembered dialogues, and the novelist's own sense of the demands of his personal audience as well as the artistic demand that Pip should narrate his own story without much editorial prompting. The consequent accumulated store of concrete experiences, which upholds the narrative and extends its consequences in space and time, remains as vital and as meaningful a component in the total 'theme' of the novel as any intellectually isolable idea or effectively remembered symbol. It seems that Dickens's vivid awareness of the need to integrate such details into the central concept of his story never flags. When Magwitch's fate is in the balance and the reader is quite certain that his cause is as doomed as his portable property is lost to Pip, the 'Jack' of the little causeway is then brought to our attention as one further, slimy comment on the acquisitive society. It is true that Pip treads the final path of purgation on the road to self-knowledge via the Blue Boar and the Forge; but this inn provides no congenial or convivial company, being but one more milestone on a journey, and the Forge (at least within the pages of the novel) is now only a symbol—no one is working there and the strains of 'Old Clem' have died out of the story. *Great Expectations* abounds in innumerable touches of this kind which suggest that, despite the occasional sentimentalism, the stretching of coincidence and the scarcely-concealed absence of any profound religious, moral or social formulation, Dickens was able to surround his fairy-tale story X with so many echoes of nineteenth-century England that the reader is almost persuaded to accept his picture as the truth.

The present form of the ending of the novel acts powerfully and persuasively upon the reader. The original, discarded ending does not develop organically out of Pip's narrative: subsequent events are hastily telescoped together and presented in a manner that is quite external to the mood of the entire tale. It records a chance meeting with Estella in Piccadilly and ends with as tired a sentence as Dickens ever composed: 'I was very glad afterwards to have had the interview; for, in her face and in her voice, and in her touch, she gave me the assurance, that suffering had been stronger than Miss Havisham's teaching, and had given her a heart to Understand what my heart used to be.' The present ending is as completely integrated into the fable-like quality of the tale as it is surely grounded upon psychological perception; the dialogue and the narrative are freshly written and, through them, Dickens succeeds in reducing his complex material to its simplest terms, to Pip's sustained quest for personal fulfilment.

For the story eventually by-passes the world of public events and social themes, although these considerations have occupied large areas in the narrative. To our surprise the end of the third Stage leads us through the Forsaken Garden towards a far from Earthly Paradise which is expressed for us in curiously negative and tentative prose: 'and in all the broad expanse of tranquil light they showed to me, I saw no shadow of another parting from her'. Pip's explorations into things past which once seemed to threaten and expose the very foundations of law and order have not shaped him into a revolutionary, but given him these modified, subdued, yet acceptable grounds for hope in a future of domestic happiness. The novel is essentially a mid-Victorian masterpiece.

Additional Reading

I *Texts*

The Letters of Charles Dickens, 3 vols., Nonesuch Press (1938)
David Copperfield, O.U.P. (1952)
The Uncommercial Traveller and Reprinted Pieces, O.U.P. (1958)

II *Biographical and Critical Studies*

Forster, J., *The Life of Charles Dickens* (1872-4)
Chesterton, G. K., *Charles Dickens* (1906)
—— *Appreciations and Criticisms of the Works of Charles Dickens* (1933)
Phillips, Walter C., *Dickens, Reade, and Collins*, New York (1919; 1962)
Dexter, W., *The Kent of Dickens* (1924)
—— *The London of Dickens* (1930)
Gissing, G., *The Immortal Dickens* (1925)
—— *Charles Dickens: A Critical Study* (1926)
Orwell, G., *Inside the Whale* (1940)
House, A. H., *The Dickens World* (1941)
Wilson, E., *The Wound and the Bow*, Boston (1941)
Shaw, G. B., *Introduction to Great Expectations* (1947)
Van O'Connor, W. (ed.), *Forms of Modern Fiction*, O.U.P. (1948)
Cruickshank, R. J., *Dickens and Early Victorian England* (1949)
Lindsay, J., *Dickens: A Biographical and Critical Study* (1950)
Trilling, L., *The Liberal Imagination*, London (1951)
—— *Introduction to 'Little Dorrit'*, O.U.P. (1953)
Johnson, E., *Dickens: His Tragedy and Triumph*, 2 vols., New York (1952)
Tillotson, K., *Novels of the Eighteen-Forties* (1954)
Ford, G. H., *Dickens and his Readers*, Princeton (1955)
Butt, J. and Tillotson, K., *Dickens at Work* (1957)
Miller, J. Hillis, *Charles Dickens: The World of his Novels* (1958)
Engel, Monroe, *The Maturity of Dickens* (1959)
Daiches, David, *The Novel and the Modern World* (1960)
Cockshut, A. O. J., *The Imagination of Charles Dickens* (1961)
Ford, G. H. and Lane, Lauriat (eds.), *The Dickens Critics*, New York (1961)
Gross, J. and Pearson, G. (eds.), *Dickens and the Twentieth Century* (1962)

III *Some Important Articles*

(a) In *Dickensian*:

Ford, F. Madox, *Great Expectations* and its early readers (1940)

House, H., G. B. Shaw on *Great Expectations* (1948)

Butt, J., Dickens's Plan for the Conclusion of *Great Expectations* (1949)

Morley, M., Stages of *Great Expectations* (1955)

Drew, A. P., Structure in *Great Expectations* (1956)

Fielding, K. J., Weekly Serialisation (1958)

(b) In *Nineteenth-Century Fiction*:

Rouse, H. B., Charles Dickens and Henry James: Two approaches to Fiction, V (1950)

Hagan, J. H., The Poor Labyrinth: The Theme of Social Injustice in *Great Expectations*, IX (1954)

Edminson, M., The Date of the Action in *Great Expectations*, XIII (1958)

Raleigh, J. H., Dickens and the Sense of Time, XIII (1958)

(c) *Other Articles*

Van Ghent, Dorothy, The Dickens World, *Sewannee Review*, LVIII (1950)

Hagan, J. H., Structural Patterns in Dickens's *Great Expectations*, *E.L.H.*, XXI (1954)

Connolly, T. E., Technique in *Great Expectations*, *Philological Quarterly*, XXXIV (1955)

Cox, C. B., In Defence of Dickens, *Essays and Studies* (1958)

Classified Index

Editor-in-Chief: Barrie Pitt
Editor: David Mason
Art Director: Sarah Kingham
Picture Editor: Robert Hunt
Designer: Michael Frost
Cover: Denis Piper
Special Drawings: John Batchelor
Photographic Research: Nan Shuttleworth
Cartographer: Richard Natkiel

Photographs for this book were specially selected from the following Archives: from left to right pages 8-11 Radio Times
Hulton; 12 Popperfoto; 13 RTH; 14 Keystone; 15 Imperial War Museum; 17-19 Popperfoto; 20-23 IWM; 25 Keystone; 26
Suddeutcher Verlag; 27-34 IWM; 36-37 Keystone; 38-39 IWM; 40 US National Archives; 42-48 IWM; 48 US National Archives;
48 Keystone; 48 IWM; 50 US Army; 52-60 IWM; 62-63 Keystone; 65 IWM; 65 Keystone; 65-67 IWM; 68 Keystone; 68 Fox;
70-73 IWM; 74 Keystone; 76-77 IWM; 78 US Marines; 80 IWM; 81 US Army; 83-94 Keystone; 94 Fox; 95 IWM; 95 Keystone;
96-104 IWM; 106 Keystone; 108-112 IWM; 112-113 Keystone; 114 IWM; 115 Keystone; 116-122 IWM; 124 Keystone; 126 RTH;
127-131 IWM; 134-135 Popperfoto; 136-137 IWM; 137 Keystone; 138 IWM; 140 Black Star; 143 IWM; 144 Black Star; 144 IWM;
144 Popperfoto; 144 IWM; 145-151 Keystone; 152-153 RTH; 154-156 IWM; 158-159 Keystone; Front cover: IWM;
Back cover: Fox

Contents

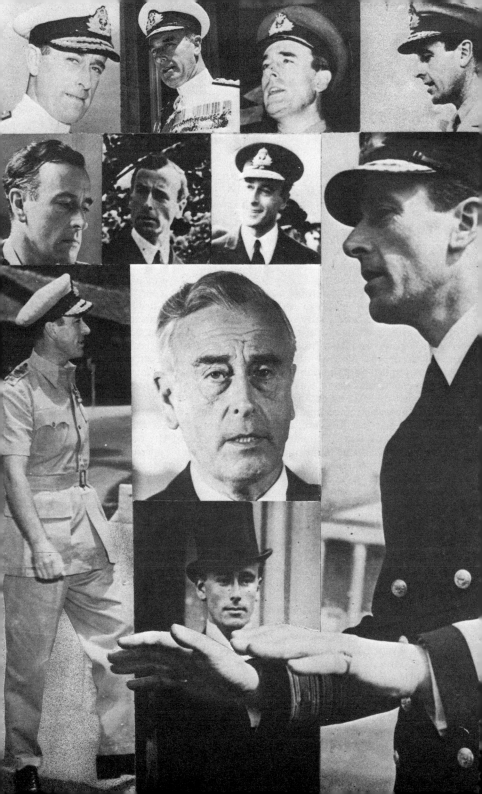

The Challenge

Introduction by Barrie Pitt

Mountbatten is a phenomenon – judged by any standard in any age. True, there have been many men who in their lifetimes have built empires of one sort or another, or who have forced their way against all odds to peaks of superb achievement in their chosen professions. But the expression 'against all odds' is so often the clue to their successes; in comparison with such figures it would seem that the combination of Royal blood, superb physique, wealth and apparently inborn physical courage (if, indeed, such courage is inborn) were almost disadvantages in Mountbatten's case.

However dangerous the practice, the temptation of attempting to define the springs of action are overwhelming. The late Arthur Swinson has indicated some possibilities in the enthralling pages which follow but possibly from a sense of delicacy he has only brushed very lightly – and that in the first few pages – over what must surely have been a powerful influence in his subject's life, the gross injustice by which his father's professional career was ended at the outbreak of the First World War.

In 1914, Admiral Prince Louis of Battenberg, an officer of long sea experience and great distinction of mind and manner, who had been a naturalised British subject since his

fourteenth year, held the position of First Sea Lord. His life had been spent in the service of the Royal Navy and of England, and it is worth noting that his brother had died of yellow fever contracted whilst serving with the British army during the Ashanti war, while his nephew Prince Maurice was killed on the Western Front during the retreat from Antwerp. When, upon a visit to Kiel at the beginning of the century, Prince Louis had been reproached by a German Admiral for serving with the British navy, he had pointed out coldly that he was an Englishman, and that in any case when he joined the Royal Navy, neither the German Empire nor the Imperial Navy were even in existence.

But he *had* been born in Germany and he was the son of a German Prince – Alexander of Hesse. This was the basic foundation upon which many interested parties were to raise a structure of slander and deceit – and doubtless the German Intelligence Services were only too willing to cooperate in the downfall of a highly efficient senior officer of the British Crown. They were aided by events. After the naval setbacks of the opening weeks of the war – the escape of *Goeben* and *Breslau* through the Dardanelles, the loss of *Pathfinder*, the early successes of *Emden* and *Karlsruhe* – it was only too easy to sow suspicion in the minds of the public, already febrile with spy mania and totally incapable of seeing the woods of overall but static naval success, for the trees of violent, and thus conspicuous, local disaster.

The suspicions were cultivated and the distrust grew – and a sensitive, civilised and honourable man, whilst endeavouring to shoulder the enormous burden of responsibilities which his post entailed, was made fully aware that his position was being steadily undermined. The task of fulfilling the duties of First Sea Lord is one which has broken the health of strong men in peacetime: during a war it demands the concentrated attentions of body, brain and spirit which only freedom from other commitments and distractions, and an atmosphere of trust and confidence, can engender.

These essential conditions Prince Louis was denied.

On 22nd September, *Aboukir, Hogue* and *Cressy* were torpedoed in the North Sea. Public outcry was at first broad and general in its criticism of the Admiralty as a whole, but with a little judicious direction it soon found its focus. Articles appeared in the less reputable newspapers upon the subject of the First Sea Lord's ancestry and family connections, his immense services to England were forgotten and those who would have most indignantly denied the rumours and countered the lies – the men of the Royal Navy – were penned aboard their ships at sea.

It took the whole of the month of October 1914, during which fateful days the seeds of the disaster for the Royal Navy at Coronel were being sown, admist Churchillian misunderstandings at the Admiralty, while the man with the rank and responsibility to clarify the whole matter was suffering the agony of mind which only accumulated spite can inflict. To say that the First Sea Lord should have ignored the attacks upon him is fatuous – as well expect a surgeon to operate with a splinter under his nail and grit in his eye. But he carried on until it was obvious that his position was being made untenable.

And then Prince Louis was subjected to the infinite malice of the anonymous letter-writer. This was no straw to break a camel's back – it was the ultimate weapon of a despicable campaign to drive a faithful servant from office.

But it took time.

Prince Louis resigned his office as First Sea Lord on 29th October and in order to ensure that there should be no untoward break in the work of the navy he did inform the Commander-in-Chief of his intention to resign, whereupon Sir John Jellicoe addressed to him the following telegram:

'Have received with the most profound sorrow the information contained in your telegram. The whole Fleet will learn the news when published with the deepest possible regret. We look to you with the greatest loyalty, respect and gratitude for the work you have accomplished for the Navy.'

It is to be hoped that these words offered some degree of comfort to Prince Louis during the months of heartbreaking disappointment which lay ahead – but it is surely inconceivable that the events themselves did not cast sombre shadows over the thoughts of his son – especially in view of the latter's naval ambitions.

That in those shadows bitterness did not breed to Gargantuan proportions is a measure of Mountbatten's stature as a man; that despite the advantages of his birth and position he did not choose a life of ease is a measure of his integrity as a person.

That in the end he filled with distinction the very post from which his father had been so unfairly evicted, is a reassurance to those of us who believe – against much contrary evidence – that Justice can be done.

Background with ships

On Sunday 3rd September 1939, Mountbatten was slung over the side of his ship in Portland harbour, with a paint brush in his hand, when the Chief Yeoman of Signals came to him with a message: Britain was at war with Germany. The ship was a destroyer, HMS *Kelly*, leader of the 5th Destroyer Flotilla, which Mountbatten had been appointed to command three months earlier, with the rank of captain. He was thirty-nine years of age: almost six years later to the day, on 12th September 1945, in the Council Chamber of Singapore Town Hall, flanked by senior officers and military representatives of the United States of America and the Dominions of the British Commonwealth, he accepted the surrender of 680,879 officers and men of the Japanese forces. He was Admiral Lord Louis Mountbatten, Supreme Allied Commander, South East Asia. He was forty-five years of age.

Louis Mountbatten aged four

The Second World War had seen the rise to fame of many obscure officers and men: but only a handful rose to Supreme Command, and even among these Mountbatten's career is unique. On this fact, at least, both admirers and critics are agreed.

His situation was unique from the outset: his family background and his rare combination of talents meant that he was virtually faced with the choice of becoming a nonpareil or a royal nonentity. To the benefit of the British nation and the Allied cause he chose the former.

His father, whom he worshipped, was Prince Louis of Battenberg; his mother was Princess Victoria, daughter of Louis IV, Grand Duke of Hesse, and Princess Alice who in turn was daughter of Queen Victoria of England. So the blood of several royal houses ran through his veins; Edward Prince of Wales was his cousin; the Tsar of Russia was his father's cousin who had married his mother's sister; his cousin Ena was married to King Alfonso XIII of Spain; and he

9

Prince Louis of Battenberg

Admiral Fisher

was also connected by blood and marriage to King Ferdinand I of Rumania, King Gustav VI of Sweden who had married his sister Louise, King Constantine I of Greece, and King Haakon VII of Norway. He could write without affectation, 'World affairs for us have always been largely family affairs.'

But if there were kings and princes among his ancestors, there were fighting men, too. His grandfather, Prince Alexander of Hesse, served in the Russian Army, becoming a general, and in 1859 commanded an Austrian division at the Battle of Solferino. His father, who grew to detest the Prussians, had come to England at the age of fourteen, and in 1868 joined the Royal Navy, in which, by ability and hard work he prospered, and by 1904 he was Director of Naval Intelligence.

It was at this time that Admiral (later Lord) Fisher returned to the Admiralty as First Sea Lord, determined to give the navy a shake-up from top

to bottom. Already the growing threat of German sea power was causing anxiety, and Fisher was convinced that sooner or later it would present a challenge which must be met. No longer could the Royal Navy lie dreaming of past glories; it must re-equip, improve its gunnery, its tactics, and all-round efficiency, and prepare for battle. It was then that Prince Louis, as forward looking as he was technically brilliant, became involved with Fisher in this great task.

In December 1912 he became First Sea Lord, and began his association with Winston Churchill, First Lord of the Admiralty. Together they formed the Naval War Staff, and brought war plans up to date; and, most important as it turned out, in the summer of 1914 they decided to order a Test Mobilisation of the Reserve Fleet. Fortunately, Prince Louis took the decision to keep the fleet in being – holding the reservists – when it became obvious to him that the world was sliding into war. And on 4th August, when war actually came, he was able to report to the King: 'We have the drawn sword in our hand.'

In the hysteria of the next few months, everything German was attacked and derided; dachschunds were kicked in the street, shops bearing German names were looted, public men like Lord Haldane, a great War Minister, were driven from public life because of alleged pro-German sympathies; and inevitably Prince Louis came under attack in the press because of his German ancestry. Fearing that the interests of the navy might suffer through him, he resigned, and went out of public life, later taking the title of the Marquess of Milford Haven.

At this time Mountbatten was a naval cadet at Osborne, where, he says, the other boys were 'kind and decent' about his father's tragedy. Fortunately no anti-German spite was vented against him personally, and he was able to carry on quietly with his career, though still bearing the German name of Battenberg, until 1917 when his family changed their name to Mountbatten. By this time he was a midshipman aboard Admiral Beatty's flagship, *Lion*, disappointed at having missed the battle of Jutland, the major encounter between the British and German fleets on the high seas, but happy nonetheless, and confident that he was in the career which appealed to him above all others. Already he was ambitious and determined to rise to high rank.

His royal connections, he found,

The *Lion*, Admiral Beatty's flagship at Jutland

were a mixed blessing. They enabled him to travel, and from 1920 to 1922 – after a period at Cambridge university – he accompanied his cousin, the Prince of Wales, on two tours, visiting New Zealand and Australia, India, Ceylon, Burma, Japan and other countries. This journey brought him into contact with the leaders of national life, and into high society. In July 1922 he married a society beauty, Edwina Ashley, a descendant of the great social reformer, The Seventh Earl of Shaftesbury.

In 1924 he took one of the most important steps in his life, opting to specialise in signals, a decision which stemmed from his realisation that if the Royal Navy was to become a really efficient fighting force in a technical age, communications would have to be revolutionised. During his

Left: The young Mountbatten begins a half-century of naval service
Below: His marriage to the beautiful Edwina Ashley

years at the Signal School at Portsmouth and later at the Higher Wireless Course at Greenwich he demonstrated his technical ability by experimenting with films, even trying to persuade the Admiralty that they could be used for instruction. When the 'talkies' came he worked out a system by which 'silent' projectors could be converted for sound at a cost of only £60 each. At the same time he became friends with Sir Henry Segrave, who held both the land and water speed records at that time, and who was currently working with R J Mitchell, the designer of the Spitfire, on planes for the Schneider Trophy, and he took them both out in his 43 knot speedboat to witness the first take-off and landing in Southampton water.

In 1927, having come out top of the Higher Wireless Course, he was posted as Assistant Fleet Wireless Officer to the Mediterranean Fleet. The Commander-in-Chief was the war hero, Admiral Sir Roger Keyes, an ener-

Left: Polo, a favourite sport and lifelong interest. *Above:* Sir Roger Keyes, hero of Zeebrugge.

getic, unpredictable, and tactless individual, who later confessed that he had struck Mountbatten's name from the list. When asked why, he replied: 'I didn't want a cousin of the King out here on my staff' – so now Mountbatten's family connections appeared more of a hindrance than a help.

Fortunately, however, Keyes had turned up a file containing letters from Prince Louis of Battenberg, and realised that 'he had given me such support as a young man, and shown such confidence in me, that I couldn't do this to his son.' So at the last moment the decision was reversed; but it had been a close thing. Mountbatten's reaction was a wise one; putting aside any thoughts of bitterness, he became more determined than ever 'to justify myself to myself by becoming really efficient in every aspect of my work.'

Some of his energies he channelled into the game of polo. It was typical of him, that, having decided to play, he took the game seriously and used every conceivable method to improve his performance: 'I had slow-motion films made of English and American internationals, to analyse the shots. I also analysed the polo stick itself, and devised a very popular one which gave increased lift and length to the shot.' Under his leadership the navy team, the Bluejackets, reached the finals of the Army Inter-Regimental Tournament at Hurlingham – a very rare achievement indeed – and they were only defeated when the Navy Number 1 broke his leg in an accident when the Navy were leading 4 to 1.

The years 1929 to 1931 were spent as Senior Instructor in Wireless Telegraphy at the Signal School at Portsmouth, and during this time, apart from effecting reforms in training, he wrote the first comprehensive textbook on all the sets used throughout the navy. When he left the school his superiors reported him to be 'a natural leader, who exerts a strong influence and constantly inspires keenness.' His reports continued in this vein. In 1933, when Mountbatten completed a tour as Fleet Wireless Officer in the Mediterranean, the Commander-in-Chief described him as 'an invaluable many-sided officer.'

By now a commander, he was entered for a course at the Naval Tactical School; and in 1934 obtained his first command, the destroyer HMS *Daring*. This was a new ship of the latest design and he was 'very proud of her; but within a few months orders came that he and his crew were to transfer to an old tub from the China Destroyer Flotilla, HMS *Wishart*. It was a bitter blow, but he set to work at once to improve morale. He started a ship's newspaper, then entered his crews for every possible event in the Flotilla Regatta of 1935. Having made a 'work study' of rowing, he put his officers and men into training, and in September they collected six prizes out of eleven, thus winning the Flotilla Cock, and went on to win the Gunnery Trophy. Again his policy of intense study followed by thorough preparation had paid off.

By 1936 he was back in London, where he took up a post in the Naval Air Division at the Admiralty. Things were changing fast in the Royal Navy, and in the world outside. The post-war era was over, and the menace of Hitler's Germany foreshadowed yet another war to come. For the Royal Navy there was much to do and little time to do it in; and yet precious days and weeks were being wasted in domestic squabbles with the RAF. Since 1918 the navy had lost control over its own 'air umbrella' and was now fighting to get it back. Soon Mountbatten found himself at the centre of this fight, and with no doubts as to where his loyalties lay. The more he studied the situation, the more he realised that if war came the Royal Navy would be without sufficient vital machines, trained personnel, or equipment. The Royal Navy did not possess an aircraft whose design was less than ten years old; and even the best were too slow and cumbersome. Without hesitation, he used his social connections, and all the influence he could bring to bear in high quarters, to bring the Fleet Air Arm back into the navy.

He remained in Whitehall until June 1939 when, with war a mere three months off, he was appointed to command the 5th Destroyer Flotilla, and learned that his ship was to be the *Kelly*, named after Admiral Sir John Kelly who commanded HMS *Dublin* at Jutland. Launched on 25th October 1938, she was built by Messrs Hawthorne Leslie at Hebburn-on-Tyne, on 23rd August 1939 the acceptance trials were carried out, and Mountbatten signed for the ship; on the 25th she was commissioned at Chatham.

This was the very day that Stalin and Hitler signed their pact, and Mountbatten became convinced that war was but a few days off; acting on this conviction, he told his company: 'Normally we are allowed three weeks by the Admiralty to complete commissioning and storing. I have decided that it must be completed in three days. I expect you all to play your part. We have a job to do. Let's do it.'

After three hectic days in which neither officers nor men took their clothes off to sleep, commissioning was completed, and the *Kelly* sailed for Portland, on the Dorset coast, to work up. On the way there came the signal: 'General from Admiralty. Fuse all shell, ship all warheads.' The last hours of peace were running out.

So it was at Portland, when Mountbatten was slung over the side, helping in the urgent task of giving the *Kelly* her service coat of dark grey, that the Chief Yeoman of Signals brought the message: 'From Admiralty to all concerned at home and abroad. Most immediate. Commence hostilities at once with Germany.'

On 4th September, within twenty-four hours of Britain's entry into the war, the *Kelly* had her first taste of action. Under orders to carry out a submarine exercise, she left port in company with the *Acheron*, another destroyer, and a motor anti-submarine boat, to act as 'enemy'. However, a German submarine decided to intervene, and when a look-out took the latter's torpedoes to be 'exercise only' he got the sharp end of Mountbatten's tongue. 'It is not your job to consider where torpedoes come from,' he was reminded, 'you are there to report all tracks seen at once.' Then there was a 'ping' on the echo-sounding device, and the *Kelly* steamed right over the spot indicated, dropping a pattern of depth charges, and the *Acheron* followed suit. Circling round, the destroyers searched for signs of wreckage, and were gratified to observe some patches of oil on the

1936, and the rank of Commander

16

surface.

For the next few months she carried out a variety of duties, escorting convoys up and down the Channel, hunting U-boats, picking up survivors from the aircraft-carrier *Courageous*, which was hit by torpedoes, and making a dash to Le Havre to pick up the Duke and Duchess of Windsor. During this time the second ship in the flotilla, the *Kingston*, began her working up trials, but these were interrupted by calls to hunt U-boats and by other duties.

The next major incident occurred in December when the *Kelly* returned to the Tyne. Here one evening the ship's company heard the voice of 'Lord Haw-Haw' (the traitor, William Joyce) who said: 'And where is your Lord Louis Mountbatten? You mustn't imagine we don't know. We do. He is on the Tyne. But he will never leave it.' That day four ships were blown up at the mouth of the Tyne, and the *Kelly* was ordered to go out with other available destroyers to find the submarine responsible.

Convinced that mines and not a submarine had been responsible, Mountbatten rang the admiral to try to get the order cancelled; as he pointed out, the submarine – if it existed at all – would have gone, and to take destroyers into the area before the mines had been cleared would be very dangerous. The admiral replied that the order had come down from the Commander-in-Chief, Scotland, and later rang back to add: 'He says "Don't bellyache" – get on with your orders.' So the *Kelly* headed down river, with the *Mohawk* half a mile astern, and, as Mountbatten recorded, 'It was a very funny feeling, creeping along, waiting for something to happen.' Before very long it did: making for two of the merchantmen who were now sinking, Mountbatten heard a mine grating along the bottom. First it was under the bridge, then worked its way aft to the wardroom, and when it had reached the propellers and was about to drift

HMS *Courageous*

clear, went off with a tremendous explosion. The whole ship was shaken, the propellers were twisted, and the stern was wrenched several feet out of line. Mountbatten thus found himself with his ship stopped and useless in the middle of a mine-field. Fortunately, however, she was able to remain afloat and he soon obtained a tow back to harbour. To their surprise and delight the ship's crew found themselves on leave for Christmas, with their fares home paid by Lady Mountbatten.

Before this, however, there was an incident which illustrated in a re-markable manner Mountbatten's ideas on discipline and leadership. When the mine had been grating under the ship, a young seaman had given way to panic and had deserted his post. Brought before Mountbatten, he was asked if he knew what the punishment was, and replied, 'Death, Sir'. But instead of being sent for court-martial as he expected, the seaman heard Mountbatten order, 'Case remanded. Clear Lower Deck.'

Addressing the ship's company, Mountbatten explained what had happened then added that he was dismissing the case with two cautions – one for the culprit and one for him-self. The second caution was 'for having failed to impress myself sufficiently in three months on all of you, for you to know that I would never tolerate such behaviour. No-body will ever again leave their post. I will never give the order "Abandon Ship". The only way we will ever leave the ship is if she sinks under our feet.'

To some, such a gesture might appear foolhardy or theatrical, but there are occasions when a leader may judge it necessary to indulge in theatricality to make his point. Certainly Mountbatten's behaviour was justified, for from this moment onward no member of the *Kelly*'s crew ever let him down; and the adventures to come were to prove a stern test of both courage and en-durance.

The last of the Kelly

In April 1940 the British indulged in one of their first forays on to the Continent – a foray which proved abortive and which narrowly avoided disaster. Worried by the flow of iron ore from Narvik on northern Norway down the Inner Leads to Germany, the British government decided to occupy certain strategic areas, to prevent German occupation. Not for the first time, however, the British were forestalled by Hitler, who invaded Norway in a lightning campaign; and before long it was obvious that if the forces under General Carton de Wiart were not soon evacuated, they would be forced to surrender.

So on 29th April, Mountbatten was given a mixed flotilla of four British destroyers and one French and ordered to sail from Scapa Flow to Namsos. It was a difficult journey; only the fog hid the ships from the German planes, and the fog itself proved a major hazard, especially as the

Kelly, **badly damaged but still afloat**

destroyers crawled up the Norwegian coastline. On one occasion when it suddenly cleared, Mountbatten found that the *Kelly* was heading straight for some rocks only two hundred yards away. Hurriedly he changed course, missing disaster by a few yards.

Above the fog the German aircraft could be heard in their continued search; and the most dangerous part of the operation was still to come – the dash up the narrow fjord to Namsos, and the return home. It was foggy all the way up the fjord, but the ships' masts being visible above the fog layer, the flotilla suffered from the attentions of the Luftwaffe all the way. No direct hits were scored, but there were several near-misses, and twenty-three men were killed or wounded.

As they approached Namsos, the ships suddenly shot out into clear water and ahead the town could be seen burning in the darkness. With the bombers closing in like a pack of wolves, the destroyers raced at twenty-six knots towards the harbour, swerving violently to avoid blazing wrecks. On the jetties 6,000 troops were lining up, and two of the transports which had accompanied Mountbatten's force went alongside to take them aboard. Meanwhile, the destroyers picked up small groups and ferried them to the cruiser *York* before taking off the remainder of the main body themselves. In all, the operation took four hours. At 0220 hours the destroyers ran down the fjord towards the open sea, realising that when daylight came the whole fury of the bombers would be loosed on them.

But at 0430 hours the first bombers appeared. The ships were drawn up in single line, the rear being brought up by an anti-aircraft cruiser, the *Carlisle*, and it was during the third attack that the first ship in Mountbatten's group was hit, a French destroyer named the *Bison*. When the other destroyers turned back to rescue the survivors who were being machine gunned in the water, the *Afridi* was hit by two heavy bombs and capsized, going down with the loss of a hundred men. In this operation the Germans were using Stuka dive-bombers, which the men of the *Kelly* saw for the first time. However, they kept their heads, and the gunners on the pom-pom brought down their first plane.

After a journey which seemed to last for ever, Mountbatten took the *Kelly* and what was left of his force to Scapa Flow. As Winston Churchill was to remark a few months later, 'Wars are not won by evacuations', and so far as the prestige of British arms was concerned, the Norway operation had little to recommend it.

But Mountbatten had shown himself to be a brilliant leader under fire and a few days later this reputation was further increased. Mountbatten was now ordered to join forces with the cruiser *Birmingham* and a destroyer force, and make for the island of Silt, in order to intercept and destroy a force of German E-boats and a minelayer, said to be operating in the area.

At about 1800 hours the *Kandahar* reported that she had contacted a submarine, and the *Kelly* joined her in the hunt. After an attack with depth-charges had proved unsuccessful, however, Mountbatten decided to rejoin the main force and with the *Kandahar* and another destroyer, the *Bulldog*, steamed at full speed to rejoin the main force.

At 2230 hours, when Mountbatten was getting anxious about his fuel reserves, and the main force had still not been contacted, the lookout called out: 'Torpedo track port.' Turning, Mountbatten saw the track heading straight for the ship, then apparently going right underneath; hastily he congratulated himself on the fact that the torpedo had run too low, but at that moment, he saw a motor-torpedo-boat disappearing into the mist. Before he could give an order to the guns, there was a loud explosion and the *Kelly* gave a lurch. A second torpedo had exploded, tearing a vast hole in number one boiler room. For the second time the *Kelly* had become a 'sitting duck'.

Though the *Kandahar* was on hand (the officer of the watch incidentally was David, 3rd Marquess of Milford Haven and Mountbatten's nephew) her captain was of the opinion that nobody could have survived such an explosion, and it was the *Bulldog* who came up and asked what she could do. To this question Mountbatten signalled: 'Take us in tow', and another long journey home began. When he was at last able to take stock of his ship he was astonished she was still afloat. Around the gaping hole in the side men were laying dead or wounded; the forward boiler had been hurled aft, and to starboard both boiler rooms and the after messdeck were full of water. The ship was listing to starboard; she had no power, and only emergency lighting.

Obviously one of the first tasks was

to lighten ship; depth-charges were set as 'safe' and thrown overboard, torpedoes were fired 'set to sink', and all boats were cast off except the whaler, which was towed. Through his megaphone Mountbatten gave the order, 'Don't jump over the side until I give the order. The ship is not sinking.' This was true, and indeed the Kelly was soon made as seaworthy as a half water-logged ship could be. She was making progress – however slowly – towards Scapa Flow.

But her troubles were by no means at an end. At midnight, Mountbatten heard the sound of an E-boat coming up at full-speed. Bouncing off the Bulldog, she came at the Kelly with her 20mm gun firing, sheering off some of the davits which were by now awash, but not doing further damage. To his relief Mountbatten saw her roar off into the night.

Later, as the wounded were being passed to the Kandahar – which had by now learned that the Kelly was still afloat – the Stukas came into the attack. Ships of the main force had come up by now and the first attack was driven off, but again and again the Stukas came back.

At this point, as the bombs fell around him, Mountbatten received a signal from the admiral, advising him that Hitler had now attacked the Low Countries, and suggesting that to release the ships now escorting him, Mountbatten should scuttle his ship.

He signalled back: 'I absolutely refuse to scuttle. We don't want any help. We have enough ammunition to defend ourselves. Please send a tug to complete the tow.'

In due course a tug was despatched, but the night before it appeared the Kelly nearly went down after all. The sea had been getting up and the ship developed an unhealthy movement;

HMS *Kelly* returns to service after repair

Mountbatten knew that if any stability was to be retained, he must get rid of yet more topweight, so the whole ship's company was transferred to other destroyers, the German planes strafing the open boats as they went across.

Next morning as the tug appeared for the last lap, six officers and twelve men were ferried back on board to handle the ship and man its light weapons and when the Stukas came back for another attempt to sink the ship, Mountbatten was manning a 0.5-inch multiple machine-gun. Though he did not make a 'kill', the ship still survived, and after ninety-one hours in tow reached the Tyne, where she was taken into dry dock. Here, when the water was drained away and the full extent of the damage could be seen, Mountbatten, and everyone else who saw the *Kelly*, was astounded that she should have survived at all. The ship's designer A P Cole came on board to take measurements and reported that if Mountbatten had not removed the ship's company when he did the extra topweight would have caused the ship to capsize that night.

During the six months of *Kelly*'s refit, Mountbatten continued his active naval service. Leading the flotilla in other ships, he took part in the bombardment of Cherbourg, and fought a number of actions against German destroyers. In one of these, during which he led from the *Javelin*, he suffered the indignity of losing both the bow and the stern of his ship through torpedo strikes, but even so managed to get the middle section home.

Throughout the fleet, his name was becoming synonymous with dash, daring, and incredible luck, though how long the luck would last was anyone's guess; but it was generally agreed that if Mountbatten could long survive the recommissioning of the *Kelly*, he would be very lucky indeed. One illuminating remark which gained widespread currency was made by Admiral Sir James Somerville, who said: 'I know of no-one I would rather be with in a tight corner than Dickie Mountbatten, and I know of no-one who would get me into one quicker.'

She was recommissioned in November 1940 and ordered to join the Mediterranean Fleet under Admiral Cunningham.

The situation in the Mediterranean was now tense, for Italy had come into the war against the Allies, and the Royal Navy was outgunned and outnumbered. Cunningham's task was to defend the Middle East, with its precious oil fields, and to keep the door open to India and the Far East – at the same time keeping a wary eye open for possible Axis excursions into the Baltic. All the time, he knew that while Mussolini was building up his forces in Tunisia for an advance on Cairo and the Suez canal.

But in December, Wavell destroyed the Italian army in Libya, and Hitler realised that if the Middle Eastern campaign was to make progress, he would have to commit his own forces in strength. It was thus that on 10th January 1941, *HMS Illustrious*, escorting a convoy to Malta, found herself coming under attack by a large force of Stukas and Junkers 88s. Badly hit, she was lucky to reach Malta, which in turn came under sustained attack. Having shown his hand, Hitler now laid plans for a campaign against Greece and the island of Crete in the spring, and determined to land a force in north Africa which, he confidently believed, would succeed where the Italians had failed.

So events began to march swiftly. On 28th March the first round went to the Allies, when Admiral Cunningham routed the Italian fleet at Matapan; but three days later Rommel began his advance across the desert; and then on 6th April came the invasion of Greece. Suddenly it was realised that the pincers of the Axis Middle East offensive had began to close, and that

HMS *Illustrious* at anchor after a refit

24

the only force which could prevent their closing altogether was the Mediterranean Fleet. The British force which had been rushed from North Africa to Greece in a vain attempt to hold the Germans, found itself outfought, and on 16th April evacuation was ordered. So the navy now faced the task of taking 50,000 men off the coast of Greece and escorting them to the island of Crete.

Altogether, the Allied situation in the Mediterranean was approaching a crisis. The need to bring in more men and supplies was desperate, but Hitler's dive-bombers had almost succeeded in closing the western end of the Mediterranean. Even the fortress island of Malta was in growing danger; and if Malta fell, Allied strategy in this theatre would fall with it.

Such then was the position in April 1941, when Mountbatten led the 5th Flotilla east from Gibraltar, expecting a hazardous journey. In the event, however, he was lucky, and when his ships steamed into Valetta harbour, the entire population turned out to cheer them. Unwittingly Mountbatten had become the symbol of hope.

But the hope was tenuous, and day after day the German bombers increased their attacks. Insisting that half the ships' companies spent the nights in air-raid shelters, Mountbatten slept aboard his ship, because (as he put it) 'I didn't like to think what people would say if the *Kelly* was sunk in harbour, and when they asked where Dickie Mountbatten was, were told that he had been in an air-raid shelter.'

But the flotilla was not in harbour every night. It made frequent night sweeps and, in an effort to intercept Rommel's supply ships, carried out a bombardment of Benghazi on the north African coast.

In May came the invasion of Crete,

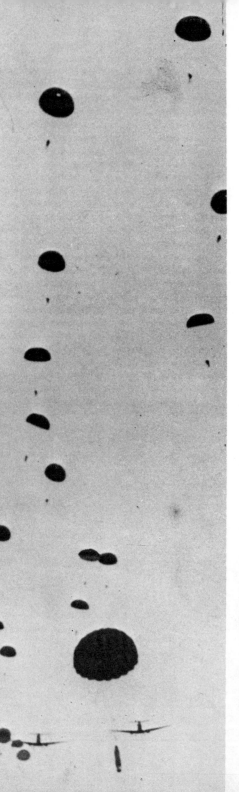

and the Royal Navy was called upon to help the army in yet another desperate situation. Mountbatten was ordered to take part of his flotilla, *Kelly*, *Kashmir*, and *Kipling*, to give fire support to the New Zealanders who were trying to recapture Maleme airfield. The *Kipling* developed steering trouble and had to be left behind, but in the darkness the other two ships approached the Cretan coast where they came across some *caiques* loaded with German troops and opened fire immediately, sinking at least one.

What happened next is best described in Mountbatten's own words, written in a letter to his sister, Queen Louise of Sweden.

'We hadn't got the exact position of the aerodrome, but worked out from a contour map where the airstrip must be. After having completed our bombardment we withdrew at high speed and came across another caique carrying ammunition. Shortly after we started firing at her she blew up in a very spectacular way.

Dawn broke as we rounded the North-Eastern Cape and we steamed at thirty knots down the Kithera Channel to rejoin Rawlings' force. As the sun rose a German Dornier 215 appeared out of the east and was engaged before she dropped five bombs which missed *Kelly* astern; forty minutes later three more Do 215s made a high-level bombing attack on *Kelly* and *Kashmir* in the face of good 4.7-inch controlled fire. Both ships avoided the bombs. I sent for my breakfast on the bridge and I continued reading C S Forester's book about my favourite hero Hornblower called *Ship of the Line*.

Just before 8 am we sighted a mast above the horizon and I hoped it belonged to the *Kipling* though I couldn't think why she had waited for us.

By now the sun was well up, the sea was calm and it was a lovely Mediterranean day. Just about 8 am we suddenly saw twenty-four ominous black objects. Their distinctive shape soon revealed them as the dreaded Stukas, the Ju 87s. They had a reputation for diving almost vertically on ships and only releasing their bombs when they were so low that they couldn't miss. They were hard to distinguish against the rising sun, but presently we could see that they broke up into two parties of about twelve each.

I pressed the alarm rattlers, for this required full action stations, and I hoisted the signal to the *Kashmir* to 'act independently'.

The first party made for the *Kashmir* and they started diving in waves of three. I could see the bombs dropping round her and all her guns were firing. Then a wave of three peeled off from our lot and started to dive. I put the telegraphs at 'full ahead'. I gave the order 'hard-a-starboard' to

Left: Parachute drop on Crete. *Below:* HMS *Valiant* fires a broadside, *Barham* and *Warspite* in the background victors at Matapan

bring the ship under the dive-bomber to force it to dive ever steeper in the hopes they would finally be pushed beyond the vertical and lose control. This happened and the bomber hit the sea close by sending up an enormous splash. I reversed the wheel 'hard-a-port'. The next dive-bomber was also forced to dive steeper and steeper and this one we actually shot down into the sea. The next one also missed.

But now to my horror I saw that the third or fourth wave had hit the *Kashmir* somewhere amidships and she was finished. I remember thinking, 'Oh God, even if we are not hit now we shall have to stay and pick up the survivors and they will get us then!'

I think it was about the fourth wave of three where one of the Stukas suddenly came lower than the others and although I had the wheel over to 'hard-a-starboard' and we were turning at over thirty knots under full helm the bomb was released so close to the ship that it couldn't miss. It hit square on 'X' gun-deck and killed

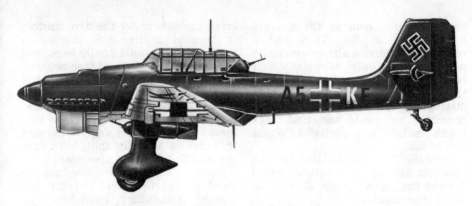

Junkers Ju 87B-2 'Stuka' *Engine:* Junkers Jumo 211Da 12-cylinder liquid cooled engine, 1,200hp at take off. *Armament:* two 7.92mm MG 17 and one 7.92mm MG 15 machine guns and an offensive bomb load of one 1,100lb bomb or one 550lb and four 110lb bombs (as a two seater) or a maximum bomb load of 2,200lbs as a single seater. *Speed:* 238mph at 13,410 feet. *Climb:* 12 minutes to 12,190 feet. *Ceiling:* 26,250 feet. *Range:* 370 miles with 1,100lb bomb. *Weight empty/loaded:* 6,090/9,560lbs. *Span:* 45 feet 3⅓ inches. *Length:* 36 feet 5 inches. *Crew:* 2.

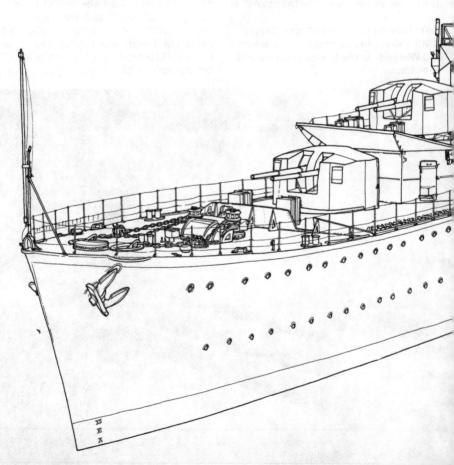

the crew of the twin 4.7-inch gun mounting, including that nice young boy Michael Sturdee, who was in command.

The next wave were coming in and I gave the order to the navigator 'midships' and then 'hard-a-port', but we only listed over more heavily to port. All ships list outwards under full helm at full speed, but this list was getting worse. I gave the order 'stop engines' and then heard the coxswain shout up the voice-pipe, 'Ship won't answer the helm. No reply to the engine-room telegraphs!' Then I realised we were for it.

The next wave of Stukas had started their dive towards us and I remember shouting out, 'Keep all guns firing', an unnecessary order, for all guns

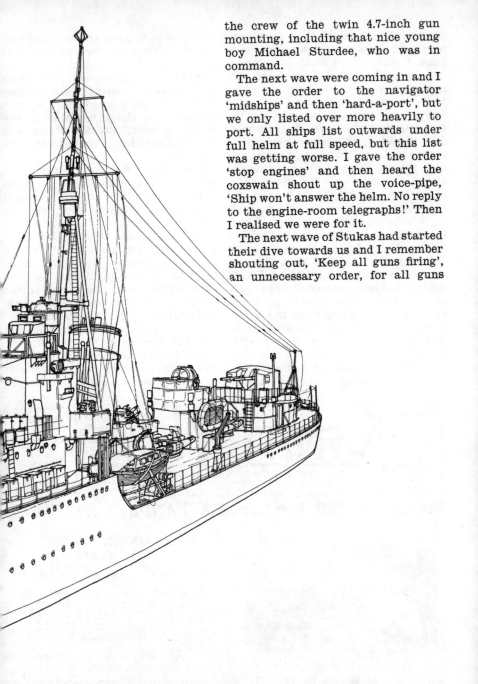

HMS *Kelly*, **K-class flotilla leader**
Displacement: 1,695 tons. *Armament:* six 4.7-inch guns, four 2-pounders, eight .5-inch machine guns and ten 21-inch torpedo tubes. *Power/speed:* 2-shaft geared turbines, 40,000shp/36 knots. *Dimensions:* 356½ by 35¼ by 9 feet. *Crew:* 218

continued to fire until the guns crews were actually washed away from their guns. I realised the bomb must have torn a gaping hole down near 'X' magazine, as we had lost our stability and were rolling right over. I suddenly saw the water rise on our port side in a raging torrent of over thirty knots and thinking, 'Whatever happens I must stay with the ship as long as I can. I must be the last to leave her alive.' We were over beyond ninety degrees now and I climbed up on to the distance-correction indicator of my station-keeping gear which I had invented and was fitted in the flotilla. With my arms I clung round the gyro compass pedestal. And then the sea came in a roaring maelstrom. I saw officers and men struggling to get out of the bridge and then I took an enormously deep breath as the water closed over my head. The awful part was that even after we were upside down we continued to race through the water, though, of course, at a rapidly decreasing rate. Somehow I

managed to flounder and work my way across the upside-down bridge until I got to the bullet-proof bridge screens. Here I had to pull myself under them and up to this moment it was horribly dark. A faint glimmer of daylight appeared on the other side of the bridge screens, but the water was churning round and I could distinguish nothing.

I suddenly felt my lungs were going to burst and that I would have to open my mouth unless I could somehow keep it shut. With my right hand I gripped my mouth in a vice-like grip and with my left hand I held my nostrils shut. It was a fight of willpower. Would my hands obey me and keep my mouth and nose shut longer than the reflex action which would force me to open them and swallow a lot of sea-water?

I had my Gieve waistcoat on, but had not blown up the rubber ring which is fitted in the waistcoat. This was lucky because it had made it easier for me to get out from under the

Published in Canea by Creforce

Editorial Office Fernleaf House Canea Telephone 400

CRETE NEWS

THE FIRST BRITISH PAPER PUBLISHED IN CRETE

THURSDAY 22 MAY 1941

Sunrise 5.18
Sunset 7.52

Vol 1   No 3   CANEA, CRETE   Price 2 Drachmas — Free to troops

NAVY SMASHES NAZI SEA LANDING ATTEMPT

BIG CONVOY SUNK LAST NIGHT

THOUSANDS OF GERMAN REINFORCEMENTS DROWNED

German convoys packed with troops and heading for the coast of Crete were intercepted and sunk by the Royal Navy last night. The convoys, heading towards the island in the darkness at full speed, were picked out by searchlights. Whole broadsides were fired at them and ship after ship caught fire and sank. Ammunition vessels exploded. The red glow of burning vessels could be seen clearly from the island.
The Navy continued their hunt throughout the night. Thousands of German troops and great quantities of stores, including guns, ammunit ion and almost certainly tanks were sent to the bottom.
No German ships reached the Crete shore at all.

VIGOROUS BRITISH COUNTER ATTACKS

Ground attack on Crete from the air with the full force of the Luftwaffe and Nazi parachute troops organisation commenced Tuesday morning. Two days later despite heavy air support of the original attackers, we are not only still in possession of the island but have the situation well in hand and Hitler has already lost a large proportion of the crack parachute soldiers he landed in such spectacular style, in the sunny calm of last two days. Both the British and their allies are fighting with a feeling of confidence that they are able to deal with these Germans now that they have come down from their aeroplanes.

AUSTRALIANS PRAISE GREEK ATTACK

SUCCESSFUL ACTION BY | THE EYES OF THE WORLD

The Crete invasion : *Crete News* reports the Royal Navy's success. No mention here of the *Kelly*'s sinking bridge, but now I had to kick hard to fight my way to the surface. Slowly, infinitely slowly, the water got brighter and lighter and then suddenly with lungs bursting I broke surface. I gasped for breath, but the next moment I saw the stern of the ship approaching us with both our great propellers still revolving in the air. They looked as though they were going to come right over us and hit us. I saw the navigator, Lieutenant Maurice Butler-Bowdon, with his back to the ship. I yelled to him to 'Swim like hell' because I was afraid that the propellers would hit him. We both managed to get clear, but only by a matter of six or seven yards.

At this moment up bobbed one of our stoker petty officers, a great character and a bit of a humorist. He looked at the 'pilot' and then at me and then produced a typically cheery crack. 'Extraordinary how the scum always comes to the top, isn't it, sir?' I looked round. I could only see one Carley raft, which someone must have had time to release before the ship turned over. I saw men all round me in the water and yelled out, 'Everybody swim to the raft.'

I suddenly noticed I still had my steel helmet on, and this seemed ridiculous in the water, so I took it off and threw it away. I pulled the mouth-piece and tube out of my waistcoat and blew up the rubber ring. That made it easier to stay afloat. Then at that moment, suddenly and unexpectedly, a row of splashes appeared between us and the Carley raft, then with a roar one of the Stukas shot overhead with her machine-guns firing at us. I bitterly regretted throwing away my tin hat; you have no idea how naked one feels in the water without one when one is being machine-gunned.

By now I had reached the raft and gave orders that only the wounded were to be allowed inside the raft, those who were not wounded were to hold on outside and those for whom there was no room would hold on to the men who were holding on to the raft

The dive-bombers came again, and again a hail of machine-gun bullets swept by, this time killing some of the men around the raft. As men died or were killed I had them gently taken out of the raft and men recently wounded put in to take their place. It was a gruesome and unpleasant business, and yet the sea was calm, the sun was shining, and it reminded me of so many bathes I had had in the Mediterranean in the days before the war.

My eyes were stinging and my mouth had a bitter acrid taste and looking round I saw everybody's face smothered in heavy oil fuel looking like Negro minstrels. This added greatly to our discomfort and to the unpleasantness.

I thought it would be a good thing to start singing to keep up people's courage and so I started that popular song 'Roll Out the Barrel' and the others soon joined in, which seemed to help.

And then the miracle happened. The Kipling appeared from below the horizon at full speed coming to our rescue. She had seen the Ju 87s diving on us and didn't think we would be able to survive. It was a gallant act of the captain, for he was obviously going to draw the attacks on himself now.

The Kelly was just afloat. One could see the bottom under the bows afloat. Suddenly she started to go as the Kipling approached and I called for 'three cheers for the old ship'. It was for me the saddest moment of a sad day.

As Kipling approached she unfortunately grazed the sharp bow of the Kelly under water and was holed. Luckily the hole was in the reserve feed tank, which meant that no water actually got into the ship.

Kipling lowered scrambling nets over her side. I told everybody to swim to the scrambling nets as soon as they could. I towed a very badly wounded man who was bleeding freely, but by the time I got him as far as the *Kipling* he was obviously very dead and so I let go.

As soon as I got on board I went up to the bridge. I was still in command of my flotilla and the *Kipling* was under my orders, but naturally I did not interfere with the captain, Aubrey St-Clair-Ford, who was a brave, brilliant and very competent man. I thanked him for coming to our rescue and asked him to go over and pick up the survivors of the *Kashmir*.

This was a much more difficult job, for she went down far more slowly than the *Kelly* and there were no less than five Carley rafts and they had more survivors than the *Kelly*. Hardly had we got opposite the first Carley raft and stopped engines than some Ju 88s appeared. Though not of the terrifying vertical dive-bomber type, they dived in a shallow dive and the captain had to go ahead with the wheel hard over to avoid being hit. Every time he came back to a raft the same thing happened. Finally I told him to lower his fast motor-boat which could then go round collecting the survivors from each raft and would be able to come alongside the *Kipling* in whatever position we were without having to try to manoeuvre the whole ship alongside a Carley raft. Aubrey thought this a good idea and gave the necessary orders.

Hardly had the boat reached the water than he came to me and said, 'There's another Ju 88 diving at us. I'm afraid I shall have to go ahead out of it.'

I shouted to the men in the waist to 'cut the falls' of the motorboat. This was necessary because the fast motor-boat is not a 'sea-boat', it is normally only lowered in harbour. There is no quick-release hook but a big steel shackle with a screw pin which takes half a dozen turns to unscrew. There was no time to do this. That is why I told them to cut the actual rope falls which were holding the boat.

A man with a knife dashed at the foremast falls and cut them. I shouted,

'Cut the after falls, you bloody fool!' because I knew what was going to happen.

I had personally supervised a course of all the engineer officers of my flotilla at the Experimental Oil Fuel Establishment at Haslar to ensure that they should be able to increase speed at a far greater rate than had been customary. The *Kipling* was no exception. Her 40,000 horse power was applied with such speed that the ship leaped forward and the bows of the motor-boat were driven under. My cry to cut the after falls had been heard by my own first lieutenant, Lord Hugh Beresford, and the first lieutenant of the *Kipling*, John Bushe. Together they leaped to the after falls at the moment when the ship had gathered such speed and the heavy motor-boat had sunk so deep in the water that the after davit was pulled right over and seemed to crush them as the falls tore away and the boat sank in the sea together with the two first lieutenants. Hugh was one of my oldest friends; he had been a midshipman with me in 1927 in the *Queen Elizabeth*. He was a great-nephew of Papa's great friend, Lord Charles Beresford. I think this incident hurt me more than any that day.

The captain remarked, 'This is going to take a very long time now. I only hope they don't get us before we pick up all the *Kashmir's*.' I replied that this was my responsibility and told him to go ahead. With great skill and great courage he gradually nosed his way from one raft to another in between the persistent attacks of the Ju 88s. But it was a long and painful business and after two hours some of my own staff officers who had been saved came to me to ask whether I would not consider allowing the *Kipling* to leave the rest of the *Kashmir's* and proceed to Alexandria. They pointed out, with complete justification, that the *Kipling* now had on board all *Kelly* survivors, more than half of the *Kashmir's* survivors and it was becoming more and more difficult o pick up the remainder and avoid being hit by the bombers. I decided that we should stay. After three hours there was only one more raft-load to be picked up and this proved particularly difficult because the attacks were getting worse. After consulting the captain, my staff came back and urged that the right decision was to let the *Kipling* go before she was sunk with the loss of an additional five or six hundred lives. I decided we should stay to pick up all we could. I felt it would be better for us all to be sunk together than to leave any of our flotilla mates struggling helplessly in the water without any prospect of being saved.

At last we were able to turn for Alexandria. The damage to the *Kipling* prevented her from doing more than about half-speed, so we limped home at sixteen or seventeen knots, the mess-decks and upper decks everywhere being crowded with survivors, many of them wounded and in poor shape.

I went round with a notebook and pencil which I borrowed to get particulars of the more severely wounded and to find out which of their families they wanted me to send messages to to say that they had been saved.

I found that my leading steward, Camenzuli, had been killed and my petty officer steward, Micallef, had been injured and badly burned. I was particularly sad about this, for they were the only two of the original Maltese retinue who had volunteered to stay with the ship when the remainder were released on our not going to the Mediterranean.

I had a word with the flotilla engineer officer, Commander Mike Evans. He had been in the engine-room when we turned over. In accordance with my strong orders no one had moved at all until he gave the order to try to get out. By this time the ship was upside down and they had to jump down feet first through the water to the two little circular engine-room hatches. Somehow or other several of them managed to escape by this method, but their experience must have been a great deal worse than ours on the bridge.

When I finished going round the men I went back to the bridge. The attack was still going on. I sat in the captain's chair on the starboard side of the bridge and watched with admiration the way that Aubrey managed to dodge the bombs. Of course these were shallow-dive-bombers and not the steep-dive-bombers, and so it was much easier, but even so there were a horrible lot of near misses. I counted over eighty near misses, some of them so close that everybody on the bridge was drenched with the spray. Her guns crew had been augmented by some of the best gunnery ratings from the *Kelly* and the *Kashmir*, which helped to fight off the bombers.

Finally they gave up the attempt and so we steamed on through the night. At dawn we ran out of fuel, but the *Protector* was sent out to meet us and give us some more fuel.

As we entered Alexandria harbour everyone who could still walk crowded out on the upper decks. There must have been between four and five hundred crowding every inch.'

For Mountbatten, despite his own survival, and the survival of many of his crew, 23rd May 1941, was the saddest day of his life. His ship was sunk, and so far as he knew, he would never see her company again. But his future looked bright: he could look forward to other commands, and other adventures – so long as his luck held; and so long as he could remain at sea, he was not greatly troubled. But his courage and achievements, his family and name, now conspired together to offer him a future far different from any he could have imagined. From now on he would quit the rôle of the fighting sailor and rise to be a war leader. To what extent his background and training had equipped him for such a rôle, only time would reveal.

Churchill takes a hand

On 10th October the following signal was flashed across the Atlantic: 'Prime Minister to Lord Louis Mountbatten: we want you home here at once for something which you will find of the highest interest.'

A great deal had happened in the five months since the *Kelly* went down, for on 22nd June Hitler had invaded Russia, so extending the war over vast areas and giving Britain a new ally, while the mood of Japan was growing increasingly belligerent, as America's ban on oil supplies was squeezing her economy and hindering her vast rearmament plans.

Meanwhile, Mountbatten had been given a new command – the aircraft-carrier *Illustrious* which had been so severely damaged in the Mediterranean and was now being repaired in the US Navy yard at Norfolk, Virginia. When Mountbatten arrived he found repairs progressing satisfactorily and for the first time since the outbreak of

Winston Churchill, now Prime Minister

hostilities he had time to spare. So he had been delighted to receive an invitation to visit the US Pacific Fleet, and to give a series of lectures about his first-hand impression of the war at sea, visiting Pearl Harbor, where, to some senior officers, his view that it was vulnerable to a surprise attack seemed somewhat alarmist.

When Churchill's signal arrived, Mountbatten was in Washington where he had been received by President Roosevelt, Harry Hopkins and General Arnold, Chief of Army Air Staff. He flew home immediately, and found the Prime Minister at Chequers where he was promptly offered the post of Adviser on Combined Operations (that is operations involving all three services). His lack of enthusiasm caused Churchill to explode: 'Have you no sense of glory? Here I give you a chance to take part in the higher leadership of the war, and all you want to do is to go back to sea. What can you hope to achieve, except to be sunk in a bigger and more ex-

35

Above: General Sir Hastings Ismay
Left: President Roosevelt

General Sir Alan Bourne, Commander of
raiding operations

pensive ship?' The argument was over. Not yet fully aware of all that his new job entailed, Mountbatten headed for London.

How had this sudden turn in his fortunes come about? On 6th June 1940, soon after the Germans swept through the Low Countries and into France, Churchill had written a letter to General Ismay, Chief Staff Officer to the Minister of Defence, in which he had said: 'We have got to get out of our minds the idea that the Channel ports and all the country between them are enemy territory. Enterprises must be prepared with specially-trained troops of the hunter class, who can develop a reign of terror down these coasts. The passive resistance war . . . must come to an end.'

Eight days after receipt of this memo the British Chiefs of Staff appointed Lieutenant-General Alan Bourne as Commander of Raiding Operations on coasts in enemy occupation, and Adviser to the Chiefs of Staff on Combined Operations. A Royal Marine officer of fifty-eight, Bourne had few resources to carry

out the task outlined in his elongated title; only a few landing craft, some Independent Companies, and 300 men of the 1st Commando which was just forming. On 24th June, however, within twenty-four hours of Frances' surrender, the first raid took place near Boulogne. On 14th July it was followed by another raid, which proved to be a fiasco, and was dismissed by Churchill as 'a pinprick raid.' All it emphasised was that before operations on a large scale could be launched – let alone the guide-lines be set for the invasion of the Continent by the main armies – a great deal of thinking, equipping, and training would have to be done. It was eight months before the next raid. But first, so Churchill decided, Bourne would have to be replaced by an officer of seniority and great prestige; a man who was prepared to fight for new concepts and a new organisation.

The man of his choice was Admiral of the Fleet Lord Keyes, who now became Director of Combined Operations. Aged sixty-eight, he had been

Chief of Staff to the Commander-in-Chief of the Mediterranean Fleet during the Gallipoli Campaign in the First World War, and on 23rd April 1918 had led the famous Zeebrugge Raid. Still a man of immense energy, Keyes was a born fighter, always fretting to get at the enemy and impatient of delays and excuses. The British Chiefs of Staff, whom he regarded as somewhat junior officers, and not really up to their jobs, he described as 'the greatest cowards I have ever met' and repeated this accusation to their faces. Not surprisingly, Keyes antagonised people and made enemies – in a job where tact and skilled diplomacy were needed.

Through reasons of history and tradition the three British fighting services had never worked well in combination with each other and still, apparently, had no wish to do so. Most combined operations, such as the Gallipoli landings, had been launched in muddle and confusion;

by the 20th Century the British knew less of the art of Combined Operations than the Japanese did in the 17th.

It was this situation which Keyes sought to correct and, from his headquarters near Scotland Yard, went ahead with demonic energy, using his direct contacts with Churchill, Ismay, and the Chiefs of Staff, to bludgeon his way through. Commandos were raised and trained, landing craft were built, and provided with crews from the Royal Naval Volunteer Reserve, new equipment was designed and put into manufacture, and ships were earmarked for amphibious warfare.

But everything went too slowly for Keyes; Britain's factories were overstretched and could not meet his demands, the army stole his troops to man the beaches against German invasion, and the navy, grappling desperately with the battle of the Atlantic, was unsympathetic to the idea of Combined Operations. So each week Keyes's letters to Ismay became increasingly strident; sometimes it seemed to him that no one wanted to get on with the war but himself. His

Admiral Keyes and Churchill at a combined operations exercise

temper was not improved either by news of the disastrous expedition against Dakar, capital of the French colony of Senegal, which was mounted without his knowledge or advice.

In 1941 as training continued and exercises were mounted, it became evident that the gulf between Keyes and the Chiefs of Staff was widening still further. In his view it was his duty to plan *and command* amphibious operations, whereas in their view Force Commanders must be appointed. They believed that the role of COHQ should be limited to the study of inter-service problems, and the development of new techniques, ships, gadgets, and craft of all kinds; and to helping them. Appreciating that the Chiefs of Staff were right, Churchill wrote to Keyes, advising him that his title must be changed from 'Director to 'Adviser', and on 2nd October Keyes replied that he 'could not accept such a sweeping reduction of status,' and was prepared to resign. Churchill records: 'I reached the

Mountbatten takes over Combined Operations with the title of Chief

conclusion with much regret on personal grounds that the appointment of a new and young figure at the head of the overseas organisation would be in the public interest. Lord Louis Mountbatten was only a captain in the Royal Navy but his exploits and abilities seemed to fit him in a high degree for the vacant post.'

It was thus that on 27th October 1941, Mountbatten took on the rôle of 'Adviser' which Keyes had spurned, installing himself at COHQ, and considering how best to carry out Churchill's brief.

Firstly, he decided, it was necessary to continue the Commando raids, which were needed to maintain an offensive spirit and gain experience, as well as to harass the enemy. 'I want you,' Churchill said, 'to turn the south coast of England from a bastion of defence into a springboard for attack.' At the same time he never forgot his main and final object: the invasion of France.

What Mountbatten saw when he first entered COHQ did not impress him. Including clerks and messengers the establishment totalled twenty-

Pearl Harbor: The United States enters the war

three, and most of the officers were ageing 'dug-outs' brought back into service. There was only the nucleus of an Intelligence staff, no planning department or planning staff and no signals staff. There was not even a Chief of Staff, and altogether the headquarters was quite inadequate for its task.

Within five weeks Mountbatten had submitted a report to the Chiefs of Staff, with detailed proposals and requests for the necessary trained officers and men. The latter were granted, and the necessary departments were set up at once, and it was now that Mountbatten's training as a signals officer proved invaluable, for the new form of warfare developing posed complex signals problems which had still to be answered. The Force Commander for any operation had to be 'netted in' with his subordinates both afloat and ashore; the army needed channels to speak to the navy, .the navy to the RAF; the leading infantry had to be able to call for fire support from the battleships, or for airstrikes from the bombers and the whole complex signals traffic must be controlled while the operation moved from sea to land.

Keyes had worked without a signals staff; as long as he had been able to send occasional signals he had been content, but as the organisation grew this would no longer be sufficient and, moreover, a signals network would be useless unless all three services used the same procedure; at the moment they all insisted on using their own. To tackle this problem, Mountbatten obtained the appointment of Commander Michael Hodges as Chief Signal Officer, Combined Operations, who set up the signal staff from all three services.

There were other problems, not the least of which was with manpower. To man the Landing Craft Tanks (LCTs) alone 1,500 officers and 20,000 ratings would be needed, and no one knew where they would come from. With Combined Ops still regarded as

a backwater (and shunned by regular officers, especially in the Royal Navy,) there were few volunteers, and Mountbatten was forced to travel from depôt to depôt proclaiming that if he could not be in destroyers he would rather be in Combined Ops than anything else. After this things began to improve.

It is necessary to interpolate here that in December 1941 there was yet another expansion of the war, as Japan launched her attack on Pearl Harbor. The resulting impact of America's entry into the world conflict was soon felt at COHQ, where, by March 1942, American officers had been drawn into discussions on the eventual assault across the Channel. On 18th March Mountbatten was appointed Chief of Combined Operations, promoted again to commodore with the rank of acting vice-admiral in the Royal Navy, lieutenant-general in the army, and air-marshal in the RAF. He also in effect became a full member of the Chiefs of Staff Committee.

Whether its enemies liked it or not, COHQ was here to stay; and those who had predicted that Mountbatten would soon follow the path of Sir Roger Keyes and retire baffled and frustrated were proved wrong. Apart from his courage and professionalism as a sailor, he was showing great technical flair, and a talent for diplomacy and negotiation.

His next move, however, dismayed even some of his closest supporters: for to assist Captain T A Hussey, the Director of Experiments and Operational Requirements, he brought in a trio of scientists, Geoffrey Pyke, Professor J D Bernal FRS, and Professor Solly Zuckerman. At all times his attitude was not 'whether' problems would be solved, but 'how'; and it did not matter how unorthodox solutions might be if they worked. For the first time scientists sat with the operational planners and helped them to formulate the questions which the scientists were required to answer.

Another of his appointments was that of Captain John Knox, as Operations Liaison Officer in the United States. This officer was to find that if the British were still far from competent at Combined Ops, the Americans were even further adrift; at his first high-level American Army conference he heard generals seriously suggesting that a force provided by the Marine Corps should be put ashore on the French coast, with nothing but small landing craft. The problems of support, build-up, and supply were not even discussed. Placed in an awkward situation, Knox had to say bluntly that the operation was simply 'not on'; and to his relief some of the Americans supported him.

It would be wrong to give the impression that in its emphasis on planning and organisation and on diplomacy and negotiation, Mountbatten's command had lost sight of the enemy. His first raid took place on 26th December, 1941, when a combined force set out to attack the islands of Vaagso and Maaloy, off south Norway, and the Lofoten islands in the north. Though the first two objectives were defended, the Germans were taken by surprise and the Commandos were able to blow up oil tanks and ammunition stores and destroy an oil factory and a power station. About 160 Germans were killed and ninety-eight taken prisoner; about 15,000 tons of shipping were destroyed. Though the operation was a small one, it showed that given the will and the know-how, the three services could work together efficiently.

The long-term impact of the raids was considerable, for Hitler became so nervous as to where the next blow was coming that almost 400,000 men were tied up in Norway for the rest of the war, and he became so angry he ordered that all Commandos captured

Right: The Vaasgo raid: an ammunition store explodes. *Below:* German prisoners

were to be shot.

February 1942 saw the next raid, against Bruneval, twelve miles north of Le Havre. Here the Germans had some newly developed radar equipment which it was necessary to examine, and it was decided to employ parachutists in addition to commandos. Again the plan worked smoothly, and after the important pieces of equipment had been removed, the radar station was demolished.

But undoubtedly the largest and most spectacular raid took place on 28th March against St Nazaire. Here was the only dry dock on the Atlantic coast big enough to take the battleship *Tirpitz*, and the Allies planned to put it out of action by ramming the lock gates with an explosive-filled destroyer, HMS *Campbeltown*.

St Nazaire lies on the Loire estuary, a labyrinth of channels between shoals and mudflats, and the Germans had installed a comprehensive defence system. The only possibility was to attack at high-tide across the mud-flats, and the course of the *Campbeltown* was plotted with great care. Skimming over the mud-flats she would ram the outer lock gate and stick there, while troops poured over the gate to take cover behind a near-by air-raid shelter. When the ship blew up, destroying the gate, an MTB would pass through and attack the inner gate with specially charged torpedoes. The troops would then dash from cover, complete their demolition work, and get away in some fast motor launches sent in for this purpose. The whole operation would be covered by an air-raid.

Not unnaturally the plan had its critics. The Naval Commander-in-Chief, Plymouth, argued that the ship would bounce off the gate instead of jamming it, but Mountbatten received support from the Force Commanders, Lieutenant-Colonel Newman and Commander Ryder. Mountbatten would not compromise on the idea of

using the *Campbeltown*, but the idea of firing torpedoes at the inner gate was abandoned.

On 26th March the force left Falmouth and south-west of Ushant attacked a German submarine, but failed to sink her. Ryder therefore sailed off on a false course which the submarine reported, with the result that five German torpedo boats headed out from St Nazaire and were therefore at sea when their base came under attack. At 2400 hours on the 27th the raiders could see a very small air-raid going on because cloud cover prevented the majority of the aircraft from finding their target. As the Germans were not kept fully occupied as had been planned the raid had only increased their vigilance.

However, the *Campbeltown* went ahead at full speed, making for the lock gates which she rammed, then stuck fast, only four minutes behind schedule. The commandos, trying to land 500 yards to the left of the ship, came under heavy fire, but closer in Newman and his men got ashore successfully. At 0254 hours Ryder decided he must withdraw, as half his craft were already destroyed and the rest were riddled with bullets. So, having fired torpedoes at the old entrance to the harbour, he set off down river with eight MLs to keep his rendezvous with the destroyers out at sea.

On the way he passed the five torpedo boats returning from their abortive hunt, and in the resulting action lost three launches and a motor gunboat. Out of eighteen coastal craft which entered the estuary only four got back.

As for the troops who got ashore or whose craft were sunk, about half were made prisoner, and the total numbers of killed and missing were eighty-five from the navy and fifty-nine from the army. Ryder, Newman and Beattie,

St Nazaire. German officers crowd the Campbeltown's deck, just above the explosive charges

Captured commandos at St Nazaire

Air Chief Marshal Sir Charles Portal, left, and General Sir Alan Brooke

Harry Hopkins, Roosevelt's friend and advisor

General Marshall, US Chief of Staff

Admiral of the Fleet Sir Dudley Pound

commander of the *Campbeltown* were awarded VCs, and a seaman called Savage and a Sergeant Durrant, posthumous VCs. At noon on 28th March the *Campbeltown* blew up, killing forty German officers and 400 men; more casualties were suffered when the torpedoes blew up the lock gates of the old entrance.

The price of the St Nazaire raid had been heavy, but it could still be counted a great success; the dock was not repaired until after the war, thus condemning the *Tirpitz* to remain in Norwegian waters.

Though raids continued on a smaller scale, it was high strategy in which Mountbatten found himself increasingly involved. Though the three fighting services still resented the formation of COHQ, he succeeded in getting things done, largely because of his backing by Winston Churchill, who was Minister of Defence as well as Prime Minister.

Mountbatten's own qualities also came to tip the scales as he dealt with and got to know the professional heads of the services.

Admiral of the Fleet Sir Dudley Pound, who had been his captain in the *Repulse* in 1921, explained quite frankly why he had been against the new organisation: any reallocation of resources from the Battle of the Atlantic might result in conceding victory to the Germans, for in the first seven months of 1942 alone, over three million tons of shipping had been lost, including 161 British ships. However, Pound, now almost exhausted by his great responsibilities, promised to do everything he could to help Mountbatten.

The Chief of the Imperial General Staff was Sir Alan Brooke, a man of definite views and rapid decisions, with whom Mountbatten had many arguments, but he was a firm believer in inter-service cooperation and slowly came to see that Mountbatten knew what he was up to. To complete the trio was Air Chief Marshal Sir Charles Portal, seven years older than Mountbatten, with whom he was able to work amicably from the start.

On 8th April Mountbatten was to have his first real taste of planning on an international scale, for President Roosevelt's personal adviser, Harry Hopkins, and General George Marshall, Chief of Staff of the United States Army, arrived in London for talks. Already, the Americans had given details of their proposed output for 1942 which included 45,000 operational aircraft, 45,000 tanks, and 35,000 anti-aircraft and anti-tank guns, apart from 500,000 field and tank machine guns. Such figures somewhat astonished the British, used to managing on a shoestring, and in turn their harping on difficulties tended to irk the Americans to whom everything seemed possible.

However, the Americans (already determined that the defeat of Germany must come before that of Japan) now put forward a plan for the invasion of Europe in 1943 (Operation 'Roundup') but they also wanted to have ready an alternative plan ('Sledgehammer') for 1942, in case the situation on the Russian front deteriorated, or (most unlikely) the Germans looked like collapsing. After discussion and bargaining, the Americans formed the impression that the British had accepted their ideas completely; while the British had only done so in part. However, on 16th April Force Commanders for the invasion were appointed and set up their offices in Mountbatten's headquarters. Two weeks later they had to inform General Marshall that any large scale landing in 1942 was out of the question.

Understandably disappointed, Marshall did not blame Mountbatten's influence for the change of heart; what impressed him at COHQ was the sight of officers from all three services working together, and when Mountbatten suggested that Americans joined the team he immediately agreed. So the first integrated Allied Headquarters came into existence.

49

On a day-to-day working level great steps were being made; barriers of language, terminology, procedure, and tradition were broken down between the two nations, as already they had been between the three British services; mistrust was replaced by confidence, and suspicion by friendship. This was real progress. But on a higher level progress appeared more difficult, and British and American politicians and commanders tried and failed to communicate with the necessary precision. So on 3rd June Mountbatten found himself in Washington, charged with what he later called 'my most important task in the whole war.' This was to persuade Roosevelt and his advisers that, with twenty-five divisions deployed in France, the Germans could deal with any forces the Allies could land in France without withdrawing a man from the Russian front. The crucial factor, he pointed out, was the Allies' lack of landing craft and landing ships – the specialised armada needed for a modern amphibious operation. Much against Mountbatten's wishes, Roosevelt saw him in private, with the result that Henry Stimson, the Secretary for War, and the Chiefs of Staff, became suspicious that he was 'putting one over'. This impression Mountbatten had to work hard to dispel.

Roosevelt, as usual, grasped the realities of the situation at once: any cross-Channel invasion in 1942 was out of the question. This led him to consider what could be done instead – and his mind turned to an idea which he had already discussed with Churchill: the possibility of invading the coast of French North Africa. No decisions were taken, but by the time Mountbatten left the United States, Roosevelt was warming to the idea. He was also coming to the conclusion – against his own Chiefs of Staff – that the invasion of France might not be possible even in 1943.

Generals Patton and Eisenhower

Mountbatten's visit had prepared the way for the next Anglo-American meeting in July. This began on the 16th when Hopkins, Marshall and Admiral King arrived with a directive from Roosevelt that within one week they must come to agreement with the British on definite plans for 1942 and tentative plans for 1943. It did not take long to dispose of 'Sledgehammer' and to agree that plans for 'Round up' should continue. Then the African operation, now called 'Torch', was discussed and agreed upon; it would take place not later than 30th October. The Allied Commander-in-Chief for the operation would be General Dwight Eisenhower.

Mountbatten had met 'Ike', when he had come to England as a planner, and during an informal conference, Ike had given his view that whoever commanded the cross-Channel assault, must be free to plan for all three services. When asked whom he had in mind, he had replied:

'In America I have heard much of a man who has been intensively studying amphibious operations for many months. I understand that his position is Chief of Combined Operations, and I think his name is Admiral Mountbatten. I have heard that he is vigorous, intelligent and courageous, and if the operation is to be staged initially with British forces predominating, I assume he could do the job.'

For a moment there was an embarrassed silence, after which Sir Alan Brooke had turned to Ike and said, 'General, I don't think you've met Admiral Mountbatten. That is he opposite you.'

Seldom can two commanders have made a happier start to their association, and on the day Eisenhower was appointed to command 'Torch', Mountbatten put all the planning resources of COHQ at his disposal. When he asked for help from the Intelligence and Experimental departments, these were placed at his disposal also, some of the planners went on loan to the Allied Staff, which became a truly international body, and Ike – following Mountbatten's example – laid down that though officers were free in argument to use the expletives customary to them, national connotations were forbidden: 'old bastard' or 'sonofabitch' were in order; 'American bastard' or 'British sonofabitch' meant that someone lost their job.

Early on it was decided that the assault on Casablanca (other landings being at Oran and Algiers) would be an all-American show, and the Military Commander would be Major-General George S Patton. This fire-eating warrior found himself offered a British-American Combined Ops planning team, which he eagerly accepted and put to work. Also from COHQ, Mountbatten lent Robert Henriques, the novelist, with whom Patton was to remain friends for the rest of his life.

By the summer of 1942 Mountbatten had established, shaped, and trained Combined Operations Command to such a degree that not only

Part of the cost of Dieppe

was its existence taken for granted, but it had become an essential part of the Allied war machine. This is what he had intended from the beginning. Unlike Sir Roger Keyes, he did not claim to command every operation; he was content to be a specialist adviser. In this he showed both wisdom and subtlety; and where Keyes had failed he succeeded.

The future still held disappointments and setbacks, however, – a major example being the Dieppe raid of 19th August 1942. The object of this exercise was to gain experience, test certain tactical conceptions, and learn about the real job of breaching what Hitler called the 'Atlantic Wall'. In discussions beforehand Dieppe seemed the obvious target, possessing an excellent port, with good rail and road communications and an airfield. In the harbour lay invasion barges, and while strong enough to present an adequate test, the defences were thought to be far from impregnable. Unfortunately, however, air photographs failed to reveal the machine gun nests hollowed out of the chalk cliffs; and the planners had failed to

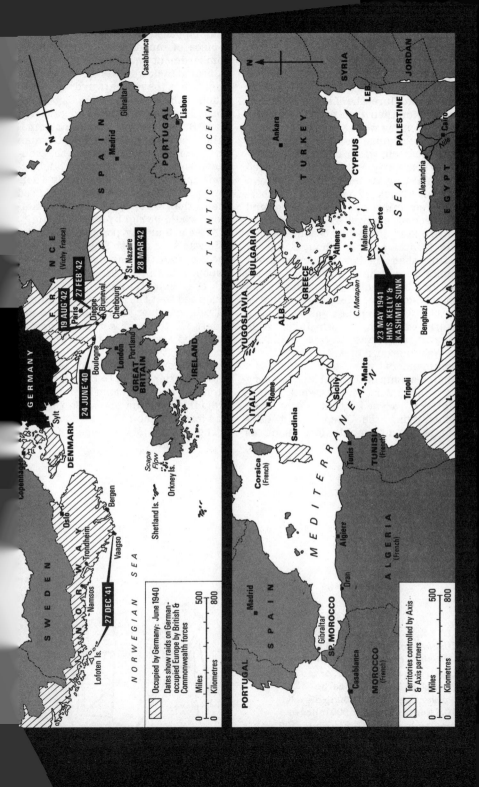

Map 1 (left panel)

SWEDEN

N O R W A Y

Namsos
Lofoten Is. — **27 DEC '41**
Vaagso
Trondheim
Bergen
Oslo

DENMARK
Copenhagen
Sylt

GERMANY

Shetland Is.
Orkney Is.
Scapa Flow

N O R W E G I A N   S E A

London
Portland
GREAT BRITAIN
Boulogne

IRELAND

24 JUNE '40

Cherbourg
Dieppe
Bruneval
Paris
27 FEB '42
19 AUG '42

F R A N C E
(Vichy France)

St. Nazaire
28 MAR '42

SPAIN
Madrid
Gibraltar
Lisbon
PORTUGAL

A T L A N T I C   O C E A N

Casablanca

Occupied by Germany: June 1940

Dates show raids on German-occupied Europe by British & Commonwealth forces

Miles 500
Kilometres 800

Map 2 (right panel)

N

PORTUGAL
Madrid
S P A I N

Gibraltar
SP. MOROCCO
Casablanca
MOROCCO
(French)

Oran
Algiers
A L G E R I A
(French)

Corsica
(French)

Sardinia

Rome
ITALY

Sicily

Tunis
TUNISIA
(French)

Tripoli

M E D I T E R R A N E A N   S E A
Malta

YUGOSLAVIA
BULGARIA
ALB.
GREECE
Athens
Maleme
C. Matapan
Crete

23 MAY 1941 HMS KELLY & KASHMIR SUNK
X

TURKEY
Ankara

SYRIA
LEB.
CYPRUS

PALESTINE
JORDAN

Alexandria
Cairo
Nile
E G Y P T

L I B Y A
Benghazi

Territories controlled by Axis & Axis partners

Miles 500
Kilometres 800

learn of the anti-tank guns which the Germans moved out each evening to cover the tank defences. The RAF welcomed the idea of the raid; Dieppe was within fighter cover, and they wanted to lure the *Luftwaffe* into a battle, for their own private reasons.

So planning went ahead, though not without arguments. On 25th April Mountbatten was called in to arbitrate over two plans. The first, evolved by COHQ, was designed to avoid a frontal attack by landing at Quiberville, six miles out of the town, and the second, evolved by Home Forces, was to land on Dieppe beach and risk the frontal attack. Though appreciating that the army wanted their tanks close at hand, in the belief that heavy air attacks would neutralise enemy defences, Mountbatten voted for the COHQ plan, but was eventually overruled. Then, on 5th June, while Mountbatten was paying his visit to Washington, a meeting of the Force Commanders was held under the Chairmanship of General Montgomery at which Air Vice-Marshal Leigh-Mallory argued that far from neutralising the defences, an RAF bombardment would alert them, as

had happened at St Nazaire. So by a piece of muddled thinking the air bombardment was called off, and the frontal attack would go in 'cold'. This might not have mattered quite so much if the Germans had not become alerted: but firstly they had gathered from British propaganda that something was being planned, then German air reconnaissance spotted the concentration of shipping and landing-craft in the Solent, and finally their Naval Intelligence officers advised them that after mid-August conditions would be right for such a raid.

After a four-day postponement the raid was fixed for 8th August. Then on the 7th, four German fighter-bombers swooped down to attack the shipping in the Solent, and most people imagined that the raid was off. Mountbatten, however, felt that the arguments for the raid were as strong as ever, and argued that there would be no time to switch it elsewhere. Furthermore, he pointed out, the vital experience had to be gained that summer; and any cancellation might prejudice invasion plans. So the date was fixed for the 19th.

The details of the operation are

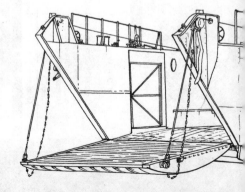

LCT (4)
Displacement (empty): 350 tons.
Armament: two 2-pounder pom-poms
Load: five 40-ton tanks, or ten 3-ton trucks, or 300 tons of cargo.
Power/speed: two 800hp diesels/ 10.5 knots. *Range:* 1,900 miles at maximum speed. *Dimensions:* 192 by 31 by $6\frac{1}{2}$ feet (loaded). *Crew:* twelve

already familiar and need not be repeated here. The bulk of the troops were from the Canadian formations training in Britain, and heading inshore they came under a murderous fire. Out of 5,000 men engaged, 3,363 were lost; the Royal Regiment of Canada returned with two officers and sixty-three men out of a total strength of 554. Many of these men were taken prisoner, but the loss was catastrophic all the same. Whether the raid should have taken place in the form it did, or at all, may still be argued. Mountbatten has never doubted that he was right; 'Nothing like what we were planning to do had ever happened before. This was the *only* experience we had to go on, and I see no way of learning the lessons except by experience.' As German records have proved, the Germans had no prior knowledge of the date or the exact target of the raid; but through a general estimate of the threats to the Dieppe sector they had strengthened defences along the whole front

Seen in perspective, Dieppe takes on a somewhat different profile; Churchill has written that 'the grim casualty figures must not class it as a failure. Tactically it was a mine of experience. It shed revealing light on many shortcomings in the Allied outlook. It taught us to build in good time various new types of craft and appliances for later use. Our bombardment technique, both marine and aerial, was thereafter improved.' Strategically, the raid forced the Germans to hold troops in the west, which otherwise would have gone to the Russian front. Though many Canadians had died or been taken prisoner, their sacrifice had not been in vain.

To Mountbatten, one important thing confirmed by Dieppe was that it was impossible to take a port without damaging its facilities; so – as a sheltered harbour was essential – he and others concerned were driven to the conclusion that the invasion force would have to take its own harbour across the Channel. So was born the project which later produced the Mulberry harbours, which played such an important rôle in the invasion of Normandy. There were other ideas which originated from or were channelled through Mountbatten's head-

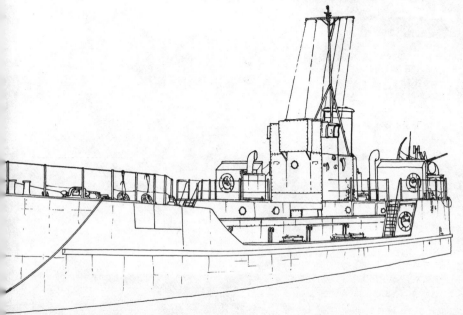

One of Combined Operations' more workable ideas. A 'Conun' is moved into place for winding on steel pipe for 'Pluto'

Sicily. Scottish troops advance in Catania, led by a piper

quarters, some like Mountbatten's own invention 'Pluto' (Pipe-line under the ocean) proved viable: others were quite ludicrous. Among the services in general, in fact, COHQ was regarded as something of a 'loonie bin', or, as someone put it, 'the only lunatic asylum run by its inmates.' But all innovators must endure such jibes; and no one, least of all Mountbatten, was greatly worried by them.

The war swept on. On 23rd October 1942, the Eighth Army under Montgomery launched its attack on Rommel at El Alamein, and soon afterwards began its great advance to the west. On 7th November General Eisenhower put his Allied forces ashore in North Africa, and 'Torch' became a reality – the greatest Combined Operation ever mounted, at that time. In May 1943 the Axis forces in Africa surrendered to the Allied commanders, 250,415 German and Italian troops laying down their arms. On 10th July came another Combined Operation – the landing on Sicily, and a fortnight after this Mussolini fell.

The news was good on the Eastern Front, where the tide had turned at last, marked by the German surrender at Stalingrad, but in the Far East the picture was not so encouraging; the Japanese forces were strung out in a great crescent from Burma to the Philippines, and any attack, such as the one at Guadalcanal only showed the fanatical tenacity of their defence.

The Allies were agreed, however, that the Far East would have to wait until Europe had been reconquered; and by the summer of 1943 the planning staff for this operation were well into their stride. A whole year would pass before that great operation was launched, but its great success portended that the end of the war in Europe could not long be delayed. A week after D-Day, when the Allied leaders visited the Normandy beachhead and saw how the long and arduous planning had borne fruit, they immediately thought of Mountbatten and despatched the following telegram: 'Today we visited the British and American armies on the soil of France. We sailed through vast fleets of ships with landing-craft of many types pouring more men, vehicles and stores ashore. We saw clearly the manoeuvre in process of rapid development. We have shared our secrets in common and helped each other all we could. We wish to tell you at this moment in your arduous campaign that we realise that much of this remarkable technique, and therefore the success of the venture, has its origin in developments effected by you and your Staff of Combined Operations.

Signed: Arnold, Marshall, King, Brooke, Smuts, Churchill.'

This was a most extraordinary tribute; but few would maintain that it had not been justly earned.

By the time the signal was issued Mountbatten had been away from Europe for almost a year; and the 'arduous campaign' to which it referred was the war in Burma. In the summer of 1943, his work almost done, Mountbatten had begun to wonder what was to become of him, and secretly hoped to return to sea. But, being sent for by Churchill, he was informed instead that he was to be appointed Supreme Allied Commander South-East Asia.

When he asked for a day to think things over, Churchill retorted: 'Why? Don't you think you can do it?' and was told by Mountbatten that 'I have a congenital weakness for thinking I can do anything.'

In fact, what he wanted to do was assure himself that both the British and American Chiefs of Staff were in favour of his appointment – for without their backing he would fail. But, as he soon discovered, not only were they behind him, but President Roosevelt supported him also. He duly accepted the appointment, thereby becoming one of the major leaders in the Allied cause. He was forty-three.

The supremo comes to Burma

Burma occupies a quarter of a million square miles, and so is as large as France and Belgium put together, or to use an American comparison – almost the exact size of Texas. It is remote and inhospitable. To the west, east, and north lie great mountain ranges, forming a barrier against China and Thailand to the east and India to the west. The western barrier runs 600 miles from the Himalayas to the sea, in a succession of ranges, some 200 miles across. Within these ranges lie the small states of Assam and Manipur, at this time forming part of British India. Linked to this barrier and running parallel to the coast lie the Arakan Yomas, separating Burma proper from the coastal regions.

As the mountains run from north to south, so do the great rivers, the Irrawaddy (with its tributary, the Chindwin), the Sittang, and the Sal-

Mountbatten meets the troops, Burma

ween, and in 1943 these were the great highways of communication, for away from the towns roads were few, and there was only one main railway line. Burma is not entirely covered with jungle, as often is imagined; large areas of the central plain are devoted to the cultivation of rice and other crops, but nearly all the mountainous areas and a great deal of other territory are jungle-covered; and jungle here means a thick, wet, primeval growth with enormous trees, and interlacing creepers, great clumps of bamboo, and in many areas, the blanketing screen of elephant grass.

The climate of Burma is a series of extremes. In the plains the heat can be almost unbearable, and in the hills the annual rainfall exceeds 200 inches; in Assam 800 inches have been known. The heat and the damp encourage blood-sucking leeches and all manner of insects which sting or bite or infect, and malaria, scrub typhus, dysentery, and even cholera are endemic. Away from the towns, Burma is an uncom-

Above: The Japanese approach Singapore. Women and children are evacuated.
Below: General Percival surrenders

ortable country to live in, and hell to fight in.

The British had annexed Burma in 1886, seeking to institute a stable regime on the north-east frontier of India. Since that date generations of civil servants and soldiers had laboured to bring the benefits of civilisation, but despite the building of Rangoon and its port, and the building of roads, railways, schools, and hospitals, it cannot be said that their efforts met with great success. The Burmese, an independent and highly xenophobic race, reacted with indifference, and loyalty to the British cause developed only among the hill tribes, especially the Karens and Kachins.

In 1937 the British government separated the administration of Burma from that of India, and the country received a measure of self-government, but this did not satisfy certain political groups who announced their intention to fight for freedom, and some of their leaders even visited Japan to enlist support.

While these political moves were developing, the British tried to make up their minds as to how Burma should be defended, and who should be responsible. As she lay between India and Malaya (another British possession), it was felt at Westminster that her defence should come under the Commander-in-Chief Far East, but in Delhi another view prevailed: as she lay on the north-east frontier of India it was argued, GHQ Delhi should take over her defence. Despite a number of conferences, no agreement was reached, and the whole matter was given reduced priority, and even in August 1940 the Chiefs of Staff recorded their opinion that any Japanese invasion of Burma remained a threat too remote for serious consideration. Only with the fall of Singapore in February 1942 did reality break into the discussions, and by then it was too late. The Japanese Fifteenth Army under General Iida had already crossed the Siam (Thailand)–Burma fron-tier and was heading at full speed for the Salween river.

The first Burma campaign need not concern us in great detail. The basic facts were that, through inaction, delay, and the stretching of resources, the British had only two weak divisions to oppose the enemy, and ineffective air cover; by 8th March Iida's forces had gained the great prize of Rangoon, and on 26th April General Sir Harold Alexander, General Officer Commanding Burma, decided that Burma was lost and that his main object must be the defence of India. It was in these circumstances that the commander of *Burcorps*, as the ground forces were known, led his men back through the mountain barrier to Imphal, which lies on a plain some forty miles by twenty and at an altitude of 2,600 feet. The troops, both British and Indian, were tired, hungry, and bewildered; they had been defeated and humiliated and their morale was low, and their mood was not improved by the fact that few arrangements had been made for their reception, and that although dangers were temporarily over, the hardship and discomfort were not.

Not only British and Indian troops took part in this opening Burma campaign; under the American, Lieutenant-General Joe Stilwell, the Chinese Fifth Army had marched south and fought a spirited action near Toungoo. Denied air cover, however, Stilwell was forced to retreat, eventually setting up his headquarters at Ledo in northern Assam.

Though not without talent, Stilwell was a prickly and temperamental character, disliked by most of the British officers he had to deal with, and by almost all the Americans. Conversely, he despised most other commanders and most troops, including British and American formations, and had a deep loathing for Chiang Kai-shek, whom he always referred to as 'Peanut'. His one loyalty was to General Marshall, who had entrusted him with his mission, and it must be

Japanese troops pass through a Burmese village

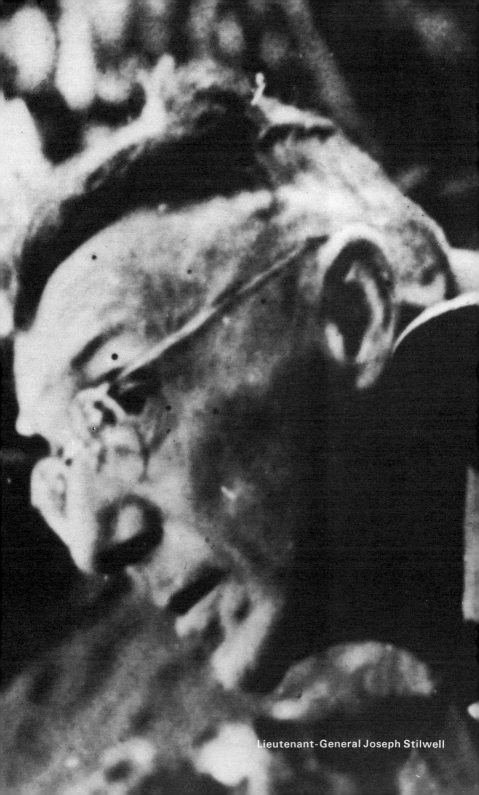

Lieutenant-General Joseph Stilwell

said that this loyalty never wavered.

Japan's immediate object in going to war in December 1941 had been to break the American stranglehold on her supplies of raw materials. Her declared political objective was to set up a Greater East Asia Co-Prosperity Sphere, dominated by herself and comprising the Philippine Islands, the East Indies, and Malaya. The capture of Burma was necessary for strategic reasons, to form a protective flank for the conquered territories, and also as a source of vital supplies, especially oil and rice. The long-term consequences of occupying a country contiguous with India do not seem to have been worked out in great detail; and there was a facile assumption among many Japanese generals that, with Malaya and Burma gone, the British would be fully occupied in keeping down the Indian nationalist movement. Even if the Indian Army remained loyal, they did not consider it a force of any great consequence.

The Indian Army had been raised in 1861, after the British government took over the rule of India from the East Indian Company, following the Mutiny. With a peacetime establishment of some 200,000 men, its troops were drawn from the fighting tribes both Hindu and Muslim, the Sikhs, Mahrattas, Dogras, Rajputs, Jats, Pathans, and many others, and there were battalions of Gurkhas, the superb Mongol fighting men from the independent state of Nepal in the Himalayas. Until well into this century the Indian Army had been led exclusively by British officers, but by the 1930s a limited number of Indian officers were being commissioned.

Well led and with adequate support from tanks, artillery, and the air, the soldiers of the Indian Army could be superb troops. But in Burma, as in Malaya, they were denied such support, and most battalions had been 'milked' of their best NCOs and men who had been sent back to the depots to help in the recruiting drive. Also, many of the finest formations were already serving in the Middle East where later they were to play a distinguished part in General Montgomery's victory at El Alamein, and the drive across Libya and Tunisia to link up with General Eisenhower's forces. But in 1942 the morale of the Indian troops, as of the British troops in the India-Burma theatre, was low.

The first ten months of 1943 brought no improvement. Quite obviously before the lost territories could be regained and the Japanese defeated, a new army had to be built up; but, before this army could advance communications (both road and rail) would have to be improved, forward airfields would have to be built, and a considerable stock-pile of war supplies amassed. There were also some formidable medical problems to be solved, for doctors examining the troops of *Burcorps* as they filtered back into India were horrified at their condition. Malaria and amoebic dysentery had taken an enormous toll, and had in fact caused a hundred times more casualties than the fighting itself.

The tactical problems were equally formidable. With their astonishing conquests over American troops, as well as over Chinese and British, the Japanese had taken on the role of supermen in the popular imagination. Could British and Indian troops ever defeat them in jungle warfare? Could their tactics be countered successfully? Could their astonishing defence systems be cracked?

General Slim was convinced that, given proper training, good leadership, and effective air cover, these things were possible, but for the moment he did not have the chance to put his ideas into practice. This was doubly unfortunate, for – as the coming campaigns were to demonstrate – he was one of the finest generals the British had ever produced, the perfect blend of the intellectual and the man of action. Born in humble circumstances, he had worked as a railway clerk before joining the British Army in 1914, and served as a young officer

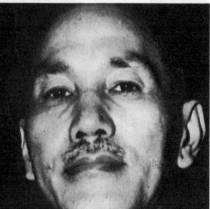

Above left: Lieutenant-General William Slim. *Above right:* Brigadier Orde Wingate. *Left:* Chiang Kai-shek. *Below:* Indian troops on exercise in South Jahore

A rubber plantation in Malaya.
Indian gunners prepare for action

Mountbatten arrives in New Delhi to take up his post as Supreme Commander South-East Asia

at Gallipoli, where he was seriously wounded. Joining the Indian Army after the Armistice, he had served with a Gurkha regiment, and by hard work and natural brilliance had risen to the top.

The reason why he was prevented from commencing his great task in the opening months of 1943 was simply that his superiors in Eastern Army had decided to take over his XV Corps and to launch a limited campaign in the Arakan. It failed miserably at great cost, and morale among the troops sank even lower, it was at this time that they began to call themselves 'the Forgotten Army'.

The only bright thing which had happened was the first Chindit operation of February and March, led by the strange messianic figure of Major-General Orde Wingate. Preaching the doctrine of 'Long Range Penetration', he had led his brigade (organised into columns) deep into enemy territory, where it was supplied by air-drops – and the fact that 3,000 men could operate in this manner without a ground line of communications, startled many orthodox generals and Wingate found himself a national hero.

But although the publicity gave morale a limited boost, most people realised that wars could not be won by raids, and no major offensive was contemplated or even seemed feasible. Strung out over tented or hutted camps through Assam and Burma, with no comforts and few amenities, the troops wondered what they were there for. No one could tell them. And they suspected, quite rightly, that no one knew.

On 22nd August 1943, Churchill wrote: 'There is no doubt of the need of a young and vigorous mind in this lethargic and stagnant Indian scene.' The vigorous mind was to be that of Mountbatten, who flew into Delhi on 7th October. Losing no time, he set up his headquarters in what is now the Ministry of Education building, and began initial discussions with the key figures whose help he would need and whose trust he had to win.

There was Field-Marshal Lord Wavell, Viceroy of India, and the political link with the government at Westminster. There was General Sir Claude Auchinleck, Commander-in-Chief India, whose job it was to train and equip the majority of the forces in SEAC. Thirdly, there was Joe Stilwell, whose position was complex in the extreme. As Stilwell noted in his diary: 'The Command set-up is a Chinese puzzle, with Wavell, Auk, Mountbatten, Peanut, Alexander and me interwoven and mixed beyond recognition. I am deputy and have to kid the Peanut into using the boys.'

In fact, Stilwell was not only Deputy Supreme Commander, he was Chief of Staff to Chiang Kai-shek, American Leaselend Administrator in China, Commander of all US Forces of the China-Burma-India theatre, and Field Commander of the five Chinese divisions in Burma.

Given goodwill and complete honesty, such a command structure might have worked; but, apart from Stilwell's deceit, all the other parties considered that there were certain matters upon which information should not be shared; and the result was that more and more the commanders tied themselves into knots. The situation was not helped by the character of Chiang Kai-shek whom Mountbatten described as 'the worst headache I had to cope with.'

Having no regard for the British or their fighting potential, and little idea of the logistical problems presented by the Burma theatre, his aims were purely selfish; Allied war aims meant little to him, so long as he got the supplies he needed. The British in turn have never had much warmth of feeling towards the Chinese, and suspected that most of the supplies which did get through to China went to the war lords, rather than to the divisions fighting the Japanese.

But, as Mountbatten was soon to discover, apart from national pre-

Admiral Sir James Fownes Somerville

Admiral Sir Richard Pierse

judices and personal feuds, his main difficulties sprang from the fact that British and American war aims in Burma were by no means identical. His brief, issued on 23rd October, read as follows: 'Your first duty is to engage the enemy as closely and continuously as possible so that his forces, and particularly his air forces, may be worn down and consumed by attrition and to establish our superiority to the extent of forcing a diversion of his forces in the Pacific theatre. Secondly, but of no less importance, you are to maintain and enlarge our contacts with China, both by the air route, and by making direct contact in Northern Burma by the use, amongst other methods, of the strongest possible ground forces specially organised and supplied from the air.'

Also, with the sea and air power at his disposal, Mountbatten was ordered to seize points 'which will not only bring about a powerful reaction but which will provide you with the choice of several possible counterstrokes to this reaction.'

If relatively clear on first reading, this document proved somewhat unsatisfactory as a basis for action, and in fact its vagueness was a conscious attempt to paper over the cracks in Anglo-American war aims. The Americans, as Churchill later revealed, wished to make an assault through Burma into China, believing that the ports and air bases in China would be indispensable for the build-up of the air offensive against Japan. Churchill, however, thought the deployment of large armies in Burma to be impossible; he hated the idea of 'thrashing around in the jungle' as he called it. What he had set his heart on was the notion of bypassing Burma in favour of an operation against Sumatra. This he told Roosevelt 'was a great strategic blow' which could be struck in 1944.

But there were other complications. At the Quadrant conference where SEAC was set up, Orde Wingate had appeared before the Combined Chiefs of Staff and the political leaders to outline his plans for a more ambitious LRP operation. President Roosevelt and his Chiefs of Staff were enthusiastic, and so it was agreed that Wingate should be allotted an army corps (six brigades) with his own airforce, provided by the Americans. His plan in brief was to cut the supply lines of the

Japanese divisions facing Stilwell and Yoke Force (Chiang Kai-shek's forces beyond the Salween), and the communications of the Japanese Fifteenth Army facing the British IV Corps based at Imphal. It was assumed that this LRP operation would be launched by March 1944 in conjunction with offensive action by both Stilwell and IV Corps. It was, in fact, on the British promise to regain northern Burma that President Roosevelt had allotted large numbers of aircraft.

When Mountbatten arrived in Delhi, Wingate was waiting on the airstrip to greet him – not with the other generals, who were ostracising him – but standing on his own. Next day, Wingate informed Mountbatten that he was obtaining no co-operation from GHQ India in his efforts to carry out his duties, and that it was necessary to issue peremptory orders before things could be got moving. Later Mountbatten was to learn the reason for this attitude: the belief in Delhi that the LRP plan was merely a bluff to fool the Americans, and would not take place. But this was some months later; for the moment he concentrated on setting up his organisation and carrying out his orders with great energy.

In brief, his organisation would be as follows. Under him were three commanders-in-chief, one from each of the three services: Admiral Sir James Somervell, General Sir George Giffard, and Air Chief Marshal Sir Richard Peirse. Giffard's formation was known as 11th Army Group, the fighting arm of which was the Fourteenth Army commanded by General Slim. Giffard, the senior general in the British Army, was a somewhat taciturn officer of the old school, a man of great integrity, and no little ability. It was unlikely, however, that he and Mountbatten would get on, and from the start there was friction. Mountbatten's relations with Peirse were not much happier; and relations with Somervell (far senior to the Supremo in the Royal Navy) were

complicated by the fact that while for amphibious operations he came under Mountbatten, for operations against the enemy's naval forces, he came directly under the Admiralty. These complications, added to the friction between Stilwell and Chiang Kai-shek, made the SEAC command structure a nightmare. But somehow, as he knew, Mountbatten had to make it work.

The early days in Delhi were therefore anxious, as well as energetic. It soon became evident that friction between the newly arrived officers of Supreme Headquarters South-East Asia, and GHQ India, was reaching danger point, and that further friction between these and General Stilwell's CBI Headquarters was adding to the complications. Many SEAC officers had never been in the country before, and sometimes (in Slim's phrase) 'showed the arrogance of ignorance.' In their turn, the 'old hands' resented comment and criticism on their past failures, and resorted to a policy of non-co operation. It became clear to Mountbatten that he must move his headquarters to Ceylon, as advised by Churchill, just as soon as communications had been arranged.

Admiral Somervell, anticipating naval operations in the Indian Ocean, naturally welcomed the move; Peirse did not favour it; and Giffard flatly opposed it. Ceylon, he pointed out, was even further from Burma and the seat of land operations than Delhi had been, and communications would be correspondingly worse. In view of these objections Mountbatten decided to delay the move till April, giving Giffard time to build up his headquarters and improve communications. But relations between the two commanders deteriorated from this moment onwards.

While setting up his command organisation and dealing with high level command problems, Mountbatten had to do something about the morale of the officers and men in his command. So began a series of tours to units in the front line and just behind, finally taking in camps and depots further back in Burma.

The routine was always the same. Well in advance instructions would reach units that the troops were to be paraded 'in scruff order', that is wearing their khaki shorts and shirts or simply their shorts and bush hats. Somewhere there must be an ammunition box lying handy, which in practice meant that the Pioneer Platoon would be ordered by its commanding officer to take an ammunition box to bits, reinforce it, and put it together again. The box would then be carefully sited to await the Supremo's arrival.

Swirling into view in a staff car, with an escort of military police, he would greet the officers with a smile, then, glancing at the rigid lines of troops in the Indian sun, remark 'Would you ask them to break ranks and gather round?' As the troops approached, somewhat amused and curious, Mountbatten would perch himself on the ammunition box, 'which happened to be lying around', and begin his speech.

Though the delivery seemed easy and even, it had been learned by heart and rehearsed. The jokes were planted at the right intervals, and carefully timed; and every line was shaped for effect. Staff officers and policemen, forced to hear the speech over and over again, noticed that it was not varied by a single word; it was in fact a complete theatrical performance.

But what really surprised them, and indeed what really surprised every officer from generals downwards, was its impact on the troops. Mountbatten really knew how to talk to them; and they were in much better heart after he left than before his arrival. Somehow – though he gave away no secret or confidential information whatever – he made the troops feel that they were in touch with the higher councils of the war; that some-

Address, from a Japanese gun

72

one knew they existed, and might even care about them. With brigadiers and commanding officers Mountbatten deployed a series of gambits, asking, for example: 'Is your security good in this formation?' and when the reply came that it was, remarking with a laugh, 'That's awkward. I tell the troops everything.'

Mountbatten's achievement in morale-boosting has often been belittled, but in fact it was considerable. Though his name had appeared frequently in the press before the war, his personality was by no means well known to the general run of officers and men, either regular or otherwise. Many senior officers, having little knowledge of his wartime service, looked on him as something of a playboy – a friend of Nöel Coward and the smart set.

Curiously enough Mountbatten's physique lent credence to such notions. Immensely tall, and with a powerful but slim figure, he wore uniform superbly. Added to this he had a regal manner, immense charm, and an infectious gaiety and to many officers who had spent most of a lifetime sweating around the hot and dirty corners of the British Empire, the charm and gaiety were somewhat overdone.

To add to such suspicions there was the immense press and publicity campaign; whenever one opened a newspaper it seemed to carry pictures of the Supremo, in white or khaki, walking among the cheering troops, or warmly wringing the hand of some local commander. Auchinleck, Wavell, Alexander, Slim were rarely photographed, and when they did appear it was in a serious, formal guise.

It was noticeable, too, that Mountbatten seemed to become embroiled in somewhat unorthodox incidents, which he appeared to delight in. One such incident occurred in December 1943 when he visited 5th Infantry Brigade, then stationed in a tented

The infectious charm

camp some miles from Ahmednagar, in central India. For weeks, instructions had been coming in to prepare the brigade for the Supremo's visit; the required ammunition box had been taken apart and reinforced. It was 1430 hours on a Saturday afternoon, and the brigade was paraded on the edge of the *maidan*, the square of baked earth, familiar to all Indian stations. The *maidan* itself was kept clear, and brigade and divisional police were patrolling the approach roads, making sure that no misbegotten driver should block the path of the Supremo. Silently the troops waited, the brigadier occasionally glancing at his watch, and the Indian sun beating down overhead. Five minutes went by. Ten minutes.

Then a dirty looking object, soon recognisable as the bread truck, appeared in the main entrance and began making its way across the *maidan*. The brigadier was white with rage. 'Arrest that man!' he shouted. 'Get that damned truck out of sight!' There was a scurry of staff officers and military police, but the truck ignored them and headed straight for the brigadier. Eventually it stopped, and as the police were about to pounce, the door swung open and Mountbatten stepped out, grinning from ear to ear. 'I'm terribly sorry about this,' he said to the amazed brigadier, standing rigidly at the salute. 'But my staff car broke down and one of your chaps kindly gave me a lift.'

Within a few moments everyone was at their ease, and when the speech was over the troops gave a loud and spontaneous round of applause, but to senior officers, there was something odd about such incidents. A Supremo should not ride in staff cars that broke down, and surely, they added, he could have transferred into one of the escort vehicles. Why did he have to choose of all things the bread truck? It was not difficult for ill-wishers to imply that the man was not taking his job seriously.

This was precisely the impression

that Mountbatten had to dispel, if he were really to exercise supreme command and make the generals dance to his tune rather than be forced to dance to theirs. Fortunately, his handling of the opening conferences was impressive. And he made it clear that every order issued was not merely a form of words but had to be carried out. He showed, too, that he would not lightly accept the army's assessment of what was impossible.

For example, on 22nd October when addressing senior officers about the future campaign in Burma, he announced his intention to fight on through the monsoon. Slim, and Air Marshal Baldwin, Commander 3rd Tactical Air Force, supported him but everyone else declared that such an idea was impossible.

'Do you know what the rains are like in Burma?' they asked. 'Have you seen what happens to roads and tracks? How on earth are you going to fly across mountains in thick cloud?' General Sir George Giffard did not argue; he stated flatly that the whole conception was impossible, and based on Mountbatten's ignorance of the realities of war in Burma. From this

SEAC newspaper

moment Mountbatten decided that Giffard would have to go.

But, apart from tactical and strategic matters, Mountbatten soon showed that he would not be fooled by technical bluffing. During a conference on Wingate's impending operations, the RAF representative stated that no wireless set available in the Far East would enable ground troops to communicate with aircraft and direct supply-dropping operations. Derek Tulloch, Wingate's Chief of Staff, replied, 'But there is. The Army 22 set, used by gunners, is quite suitable.' When the conference broke up Mountbatten had Tulloch's statement checked by his own signals experts, and found that it was perfectly correct. After this word went round that if you wanted to carry on a technical argument with Mountbatten, you had better get your facts right.

But apart from impressing his will on the generals during these first weeks in Delhi, Mountbatten took decisions concerning the troops which must be mentioned here. His object, as he put it recently, was 'to try and make our men feel that Burma was no longer the forgotten front, to bring news of the outside world to them, and of them to the outside world.' So

SEAC' NEWSPAPER

with Churchill's backing he started *SEAC*, a daily newspaper, with Frank Owen from Fleet Street as editor. He also launched a weekly picture magazine called *Phoenix*; and set up an organisation for feeding news of the Burma front to the British press. He set up cinema units, which went from camp to camp, showing the latest Hollywood and British films. He had radio sets issued so that all the troops could hear the forces network from All India Radio and later on Radio SEAC from Ceylon.

In a personal effort to get through to the troops he filled a notebook with stock phrases such as 'How many years' service have you got?' and 'Where is your home?' and these were translated into Urdu, Gurkhali, Burmese, Ceylonese, Hausa (African troops were on their way to SEAC), Swahili, Mandarin Chinese, and other languages. The idea, again, could be condemned as theatrical; but Mountbatten did not mind this, if it did what he wanted. Later he said, 'The results were surprisingly effective.'

Like other newcomers, he was shocked at the state of the troops who had come out of Burma, and realised that a major effort must be made in the medical field. With the help of all three services and the Americans he set up a Medical Advisory Division on Tropical Diseases, and this rapidly began attacking the problems of malaria, cholera, dysentery, and scrub typhus. Soon all the troops were being issued with mepacrine tablets to ward off malaria, and a flow of advice went out to unit doctors, field ambulances, and hospitals. The results of this campaign were remarkable, and later on were to pay off in battle. The Japanese had no medical research units and their casualties from disease were far higher as a consequence.

So in November 1943 the whole of the Fourteenth Army, and indeed the fighting services throughout SEAC, were preparing themselves for battle. But where would the battle be fought? And when? And in what form? As Mountbatten was becoming increasingly aware, the answers provided by his generals and air marshals were increasingly vague, and he was not getting a great deal of guidance from London. At the Sextant Conference held towards the end of November, war plans seemed to be in complete confusion. Long before he was ready for it, the Supremo was approaching a crisis.

Order counter-order disorder

The Sextant Conference, which began at Cairo on 23rd November, was called ostensibly to complete Allied plans for the relief of China. Before it had been going on very long, however, both these plans and the manner of their realisation came under dispute, and relations between the great figures engaged became hostile. As Stilwell recorded, 'Brooke got nasty and King got sore. God he was mad. I wish he had socked him.'

As for Mountbatten, he could hardly have been at ease. Roosevelt's assumption was that he was about to launch 'the largest possible operation to retake Burma', but, as Mountbatten must have known, Slim was not anxious to go over to the offensive. (He had fought enough battles with overstretched communications, and wanted the Japanese to overstretch theirs instead. He believed that no decision could be reached in central Burma before the Japanese armies

Amphibious craft, a constant shortage

had been severely hurt between Imphal and the Chindwin).

Mountbatten badly wanted news of the amphibious craft and naval forces essential for the Sumatra operation, but on the opening day he was to hear the American Chiefs of Staff announce that the resources were not available. What they recommended instead was an attack on the Andaman Islands, in the Indian Ocean. Dutifully, Mountbatten put forward his plans for capturing northern Burma by May 1944, to hear them condemned by Chiang Kai-shek. Unless the Allies controlled the sea, the Chinese leader argued, the Japanese could reinforce their ground troops in Burma and retake the territory captured.

In the event such arguments became academic, for by the time the conference was over, British amphibious resources were withdrawn, and in consequence all amphibious operations in the Bay of Bengal were postponed, and Mountbatten's task was now limited to capturing upper

Stilwell meets Brigadier-General Frank Merrill

Major-General Wedemeyer gets out among the Chinese

Burma by the spring of 1944, 'to improve the air route and establish overland communications with China.' So on 14th January 1944 he issued a directive to his Commanders-in-Chief which cancelled all previous and more ambitious orders.

Altogether there were to be four small operations: an advance in the Arakan towards the port of Akyab, a limited advance by IV Corps from Imphal on the central front, an advance by Stilwell and his Chinese/American forces (Stilwell now had Merrill's Marauders under command) on the northern front, and Wingate's LRP operations. After a great fanfare of trumpets, Mountbatten was reduced to blowing a tin whistle.

But with the situation deteriorating, he was beginning to doubt that even these minor operations were possible. At the end of December he had sent Wingate – whose powers of persuasion were considerable – to try to persuade Chiang Kai-shek to commit his divisions in Yunnan (Yoke Force) to the north Burma offensive, but Wingate failed like everyone else. 'When you have completed the conquest of Burma,' Chiang Kai-shek had said in effect, 'I will cross the Salween – but not before.'

When Wingate proferred the large basket of Jaffa oranges sent by Madame Chiang Kai-shek, Mountbatten commented wryly, 'Oranges? They should have been lemons.'

This final message from Chiang, it seems clear, made a deep impact on Mountbatten; and though he included it in his directive, he had serious doubts as to whether the northern offensive could really take place. In short, he thought that Chiang's refusal had 'let him off the hook'.

The generals had already convinced him that Stilwell could not capture the key Japanese base of Myitkyina before the monsoon; and that it was useless to conquer northern Burma, until the Fourteenth Army was ready to take the whole of Burma. Churchill, as he now realised, had no desire to oblige the Americans by messing around in northern Burma; and the British Chiefs of Staff felt the same way. Though they were not particularly frank with him, the generals seemed to be dragging their feet over the IV Corps operations; and now only Wingate believed that the LRP operation would take place.

The whole theatre had become a pool of rumour and indecision. It is clear too, that Mountbatten was swinging to Churchill's general strategic view that if in the autumn of 1944 the Sumatra operation could be brought off, Burma could still be by-passed and a great deal of trouble saved. Recently he has admitted that 'you didn't have to be a strategic genius to see that amphibious operations – getting behind the Japanese – were the best way of attacking Burma, or that a fearful land advance straight down from the top end was just about the worst way. A lance-corporal could have told you that.'

But if Churchill and Mountbatten were agreed on broad strategic designs they were by no means agreed on the scope of operations. Learning of Mountbatten's plan for the Andamans Churchill wrote: 'Everyone had been unpleasantly affected by your request to use 50,000 British and Imperial troops against 5,000 Japanese. I was astounded to hear of such a requirement. The Americans have been taking their islands on a basis of two and a half to one. While such standards as those you have accepted prevail there is not much hope of making any form of amphibious war.' As Mountbatten was only using amphibious resources which he then had in the theatre and troops of which he had many more than he could use in Burma he was horrified at this unfair criticism. The Fourteenth Army could not afford another failure at any price – and his plan to make use of all available resources had been based on this fact.

Burma: The Japanese advance

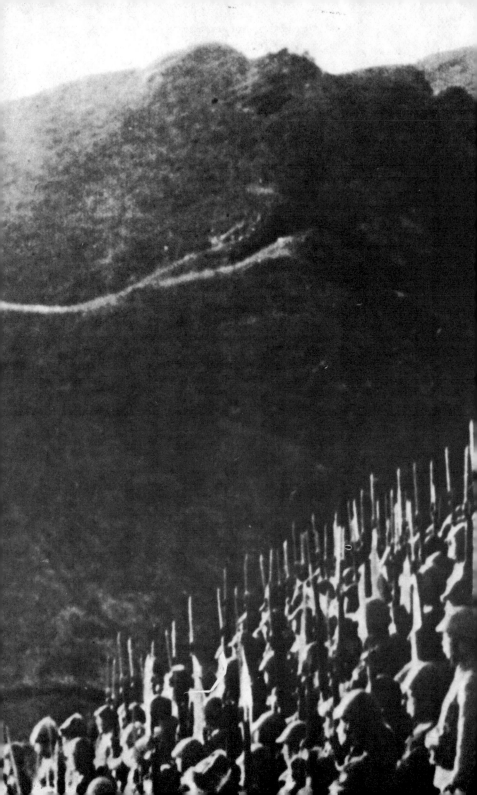

Japanese troops parade on the border between Indo-China and Burma

In mid-January Mountbatten decided to send a group of his officers, to be called the Axiom Mission, to London and then to Washington to present his views. Leading the mission was the American, Major-General Wedemeyer, his Deputy Chief of Staff, who had a difficult task ahead of him. In Britain the politicians and the generals were at loggerheads. For reasons of prestige, the former argued, Burma and Malaya must be recaptured before the war ended. The Chiefs of Staff, however, considered that the British should base their efforts in Australia and join the Americans in their sweep across the Pacific. Like Churchill, they detested the idea of 'threshing about in the jungles.'

In America, however, the attitude was quite different. The old fox, Joe Stilwell, had sent his own mission, warning the American Chiefs of Staff that the British intended to 'chicken out' of fighting in Burma. Also, as Wedemeyer soon discovered, a nationwide press campaign was being launched, deriding Mountbatten's feeble handling of the Burma cam-

Artillery moves up for battle

paign, and demanding that Stilwell should be backed to the hilt and northern Burma should be recaptured.

On 17th February, the American Chiefs of Staff made their position quite plain, writing to their colleagues in London with the following recommendations:

1. Stilwell should be ordered to advance south and capture Myitkyina before the monsoon.
2. The British IV Corps should be ordered to advance into central Burma at once, to support Stilwell.

They were absolutely against the idea of withholding forces from Burma for any future operation against Sumatra.

Faced with this announcement, the British Chiefs of Staff stalled until Mountbatten's reaction has been received. He made it clear to them that he was not withholding forces for the attack on Sumatra, but considered that, by employing these forces in Burma, the chances of taking Sumatra in November 1944 were being prejudiced. There were now eight Japanese divisions in Burma, he explained, which made it impossible for IV Corps to seize the Shwebo-Monya area before the monsoon. Nor did he think Stilwell

would reach Myitkyina before the 1944 monsoon, so enabling the Ledo road to be completed across the Hukawng Valley. And without the road, Myitkyina could not be held. His problems, Mountbatten added, all stemmed from the difficulty of communications in Burma. He was already short of transport aircraft and had been forced to borrow planes from the ferry route to China. The views of the American Chiefs of Staff, he said, were based on incorrect logistical information supplied by Stilwell.

In the event, the argument proved academic, for news soon arrived that the main Japanese fleet had arrived at Singapore. The attack on Sumatra was out. If the Japanese were to be attacked at all it would now have to be on land and in the air.

Then on 25th February President Roosevelt sent a telegram to Churchill, urging an all-out drive in Burma. He reminded the British leader of the pledges given during the Quadrant Conference at Quebec, and indicated that, having kept their promises, the Americans were now holding the British to theirs. In other words, Mountbatten was not 'let off the hook' by Chiang Kai-shek's refusal to co-operate. Stilwell's offensive in northern Burma must go ahead. And Wingate's LRP force must fly in to cut the Japanese communications.

There was another important development. On 24th March, at a meeting of the Combined Chiefs of Staff, General Arnold stated that he would agree to Admiral Mountbatten's request for an extra 400 transport aircraft and promised to provide them to reach SEAC in groups of a hundred a month, beginning on 1st July. Through the generosity of the Americans, the Burma front was taking on a new look; and an offensive on land was beginning to seem feasible. All that was needed now was an offensive spirit.

The offensive spirit was there alright but on the wrong side: on 15th March the Japanese commanders loosed their attack on Fourteenth Army. Already deeply embroiled in problems of Anglo-American war aims, of diplomacy, training, and organisation, Mountbatten found himself engaged in the desperate struggle to save the Burma front from disintegrating. He was now approaching the major crisis of his career.

mbe dell'alba suonano l'inizio della marcia verso il
orientale dell'India. Esso è stato varcato dalle trup-
pponesi il 10 gennaio. Lungo è il cammino che esse
già percorso dalla patria, e lungo è ancora quello
sta da percorrere in terra nemica, ma una volon-
ferro anima le mai stanche falangi dell'Imperatore.

PONESI E TAILANDESI IRROMPONO IN BIR

The march on Delhi

The senior Japanese officer in Burma in 1943 was Lieutenant-General Kawabe, Commander Burma Area Army, and on 14th June 1943 he held a conference at Rangoon to discuss the coming offensive towards Assam and India. On the second day Renya Mutaguchi, the blustering, energetic commander of Fifteenth Army on the central front, put forward his proposal for an attack on Imphal, and was given a favourable hearing. The plan was briefly that Twenty-eighth Army (still to be formed) should launch an attack in the Arakan, forcing Slim to commit his reserves. Mutaguchi would then lead Fifteenth Army across the Chindwin, surround the leading divisions of IV Corps, which would have been pushed out towards the river, then head swiftly for the Imphal plain. While this operation was in progress, Stilwell would be kept in check by two Japanese divisions in the north.

Axis on the offensive: Italians announce a Japanese advance

Mutaguchi's offensive ideas came at an opportune moment, for with defeats at Guadalcanal, Midway Island, and in New Guinea, and with the American Navy tightening its blockade, the Japanese High Command needed a success to boost morale. So it came about that in July Mutaguchi learned that reinforcements were on the way to Burma, and at his headquarters at Maymo, a pleasant hill town east of Mandalay, set up a planning staff. The objective of the operation, as laid down by Kawabe, would be 'To upset the British base around Imphal, to suppress the British counteroffensive, to strengthen the defence of Burma, and to exercise political control over India.'

Throughout the autumn planning continued, though there was a series of disappointments. Southern Army (the superior formation at Singapore) refused to allot fifty road building companies and then Lieutenant-General Yamauchi arrived with the news that his 15th Division had been delayed on road building duties in

General Masa kazu Kawabe,
Commanding General Burma Army

Lieutenant-General Renya Mutaguchi,
Commander Fifteenth Army

Lieutenant-General Masafumi
Yamauchi, Commander 15th Division

Lieutenant-General Kotoku Sato,
Commander 31st Division

Siam. Also, lines of communications troops were almost entirely lacking and Mutaguchi was forced to consider supplying his troops by elephant transport and by sending cattle forward. (Both of which he in fact did – with disastrous results.)

By December, although Tokyo Radio was announcing that 'Now, on the threshold of a New Year, Japan will seek to consolidate her gains,' Imperial Headquarters was proving somewhat lethargic, and no date for the Japanese offensive could be obtained. It was 7th January before Kawabe received his orders, and the 19th before he passed them on to Mutaguchi. The orders were now couched in the following terms:

1. Mutaguchi would seize Imphal before the Allies were ready with their counteroffensive.

2. He would build up strong defences covering Imphal and Kohima before the monsoon.

3. He would launch his offensive between mid-February and early March so that it could be completed by mid-April. (This would leave one month before the monsoon broke.)

Though Kohima had been mentioned in discussions, this was the first time it had been mentioned in orders, and a word of explanation would be helpful. Running up from Calcutta, the railway line went north to Parbatipur, then swung east to Gauhati, where it was broken by the river Brahmaputra. From here it continued to Dimapur, railhead for the Fourteenth Army, then ran up the Brahmaputra Valley to Stilwell's base at Ledo. Some 120 miles to the south of Dimapur lay Imphal, reached by a single tarmac road which wound its way through the mountains, over a saddle at Kohima, lying at 4,500 feet, some fifty miles south of Dimapur provided a defensive position of great strength.

Once it was taken, no reinforcements could reach Imphal and the central front from Dimapur; and Dimapur would be at the mercy of the Japanese. If Dimapur itself were taken, of course, Stilwell's communications would be cut also and the northern front would become untenable. In Japanese terms, Kohima would become 'the northern bastion of the defensive line', and so it was decided that Lieutenant-General Sato and the 31st Division should be allotted the task of taking it. In a direct line from the Chindwin, Kohima was barely sixty miles, and by track less than one hundred. To facilitate matters, reconnaissance revealed that the British had built a jeep track most of the way.

So, despite delays, the offensive went ahead. On 4th February Sakurai's Twenty-eighth Army marched agaist the British XV Corps in the Arakan. To Sakurai's surprise, however, the British made no attempt to retreat; Mountbatten had given personal orders that there were to be no more retreats as he would supply by air any troops who were cut off. News of the British stand, however, did not disturb Mutaguchi; his main concern was that there was still no sign of Yamauchi's 15th Division and only on 11th March did it march into Maymo, its men thin and exhausted, a good deal of its equipment missing or unusable.

Just four days were left now before his main offensive on Imphal was to be launched; already it had been postponed, and further delay would prove fatal. So, having heard that Slim had committed his reserves in the Arakan, Mutaguchi decided that, whatever its condition, Yamauchi's division must be thrown across the Chindwin, together with Yanagida's 33rd, Sato's 31st and an Indian National Army division.

Yanagida's division, split into two columns, had the job of cutting off IV Corps' forward divisions (the 17th under Cowan, lying east of Kalewa in the Fort White-Tiddim area, and the 20th (under Gracey), further north in the Kabaw Valley. Yamauchi would envelope Imphal in a right hook, while Sato cut the Imphal-Kohima road near Maram, then occupied Kohima itself. In thirty days, Mutaguchi calculated, the campaign would be over and the Allied front overrun.

As he realised, Imperial Headquarters were insisting that once the objectives had been achieved, the Japanese forces should be re-formed in a defensive line, but with his insatiable ambition. Mutaguchi was determined to go on as far as possible, to Dimapur, and even into India itself. As he confided later, 'In my private speculations I saw myself riding through Delhi on a white horse.' Some indication of Mutaguchi's mood of confidence may be gauged from his Order of the Day: 'The Army has now reached the stage of invincibility and the day when the Rising Sun shall proclaim our victory in India is not so far off.

'This operation will engage the attention of the whole world and is eagerly awaited by 100,000,000 of our countrymen. By its decisive nature, its success will have a profound effect upon the course of the war and may even lead to its conclusion.

'I will remind you that a speedy and successful advance is the keynote of this operation, despite all the obstacles of the river, mountain and labyrinthine jungle. Aided by the Gods and inspired by the Emperor and full of will to win, we must realise the objective of this operation. Both officers and men must fight to the death for their country and accept the burden of duties which are the lot of the soldier of Japan.

'The will of the Emperor and our countrymen must be fulfilled.'

This order was issued on 18th February. On 7th March Mutaguchi put out a signal, 'The fortunes of Imperial Japan rest on our shoulders.' – This was the message which Admiral Togo, the great national hero, had sent out before his victory over the Russian fleet at the battle of Tsushima in 1905. A *samurai* of the purest breed, Mutaguchi had no doubt that his hour

Japanese troops, at home in the Arakan jungle

of destiny had come; that if he could imbue his army with the mysterious power of *kiai* – the resolution to overcome all obstacles, and *gyokusai* – the will to die rather than surrender – victory was assured.

He was not greatly disturbed by the inadequacies of his supply system; for the *samurai* code taught that by bravery in battle such matters coud be overcome; and in any case there were plenty of stores to be captured in Imphal. He also professed himself unperturbed by news that Wingate had launched his second operation, and several brigades were now threatening his communications. To the war correspondent, Yukihiko Imai, he said reassuringly, 'These men are orphans of the jungle. We'll surround them and starve them out.'

In the days, and indeed the weeks to come, it seemed – despite minor setbacks – that Mutaguchi's confidence both in himself and in the mysterious virtues of the *samurai* code were justified. Without any doubt whatsoever he had seized the initiative on the Burma front.

Mountbatten had been aware that the Japanese were planning an offensive, since January 1944. At this time Fourteenth Army had two Indian divisions in the Arakan (the 5th and 7th Indian, both battle-hardened formations) and the 81st West African, which comprised Christison's XV Corps. At Imphal, Scoones's IV Corps consisted of three divisions, the 17th, 20th and 23rd Indian, of which two (as already noted) were in advanced positions covering the Chindwin. If not considerable, these were stronger forces than had been pushed out of Burma in 1942, and they enjoyed effective air cover, and had medium tank brigades in support.

The six brigades allocated to Wingate's coming operation were still training in India. As Mountbatten was aware, Slim was against the employment of such large forces in a specialised role, and indeed against 'private armies' of any kind.

Throughout January there was a steady build-up of Intelligence information reaching SEAC headquarters. Air reconnaissance reported that rafts were being concealed in the lower reaches of the Uyu river, opposite Homalin on the Chindwin, and herds of cattle were being concentrated not far away at Thaungdut, also on the Chindwin. Agents from 'V' Force, the Intelligence screen, also brought in stories of 'the massing of transport, both mechanical and animal, and even including elephants.'

By the end of January Mountbatten had in his possession a fairly comprehensive picture of the whole Japanese order of battle. The enemy intentions, so the forecasts given him stated, were to capture Imphal then break through to the Brahmaputra Valley in order to cut off Stilwell and disrupt the air supply to China. It was estimated that one Japanese regiment (equivalent to a British brigade) would head for Kohima, cut the road to Imphal, and threaten the Imphal base. The estimated date for the offensive to begin was 15th March.

How would this threat be answered? Mountbatten now learned from Slim that in his view the Allied forces covering Assam were inadequate; in due course, therefore, he proposed to bring up the 5th and 7th Divisions from the Arakan, and replace them with new formations from India. But when this idea was put to the Movements Control staff at Giffard's 11th Army Group, they said it would be impossible: the divisions would have to stay where they were, and (if fresh troops were really needed) the 2nd British Division and the 50th Indian Parachute Brigade would have to be sent direct from India to Dimapur.

By the beginning of March, by which time the Japanese Arakan offensive had shot its bolt, it became clear that new formations *would* be needed – and more than at first calculated. On 5th March, having watched Wingate's

Mutaguchi visits front-line troops. One dons his helmet

Mountbatten also visits forward areas: The RAF on the Arakan Front

R AAF Thunderbolts on a forward airfield : Arakan Front

Japanese Fifteenth Army troops across the Chindwin

leading brigades fly in (a third brigade was marching south from Ledo), Slim asked for the 25th and 26th Indian Divisions to be brought into the theatre. These would relieve the 5th Division which would then be moved from the Arakan to Assam. It began to look very much that instead of calmly awaiting the Japanese thrust, the Allied generals were now shuffling their formations about in order to plug the gaps.

Day by day more information poured into Mountbatten's headquarters of the rapid development of the Japanese offensive. On the 8th the 215th Regiment was crossing the Manipur river, several miles to the south of Tiddim. On the 9th a column was located at a point fifteen miles to the west of Tiddim. And on the 10th Cowan's 17th Division, having orders to defend Tiddim at all costs, began digging in. On the 12th reports came in of Sato's advance towards Kohima. And on the 13th, when it was almost too late, Scoones ordered Cowan to withdraw to the Imphal Plain. But already Yanagida's column had cut the road back, so that Scoones was forced to despatch his only reserves to extricate them. So it was now imperative that the 5th Division should be expedited from the Arakan to Imphal.

Altogether the campaign was opening very untidily for the British, and only in the Arakan were things going well. Here Sakurai, as Mount-

batten reported later, 'was faced with a complete breakdown of his adminis- trative system. For the whole opera- tion was based on the assumption that he would be able to bring about the wholesale retirement of our forces by infiltration and outflanking movements – as in the past. (But our) units had all been ordered to stand firm; and they did so.' Ordered to block all tracks to close the enemy's escape, 7th Division had succeeded to a remarkable degree; and from the last week of February the Japanese were forced to break up into small groups to get past. On 11th March, 7th Divi- sion went over to the offensive, cap- turing Buthidaung; and in the Kaladan Valley inland, 81st West African Division contained a large part of the 54th Division. But despite such suc- cesses, it had to be recognised that less than two Japanese divisions were tying down five British-Indian divi- sions, including those moving up in relief.

Unfortunately for Mountbatten, at this critical phase of the campaign, he was in hospital for four days. On 5th March, being concerned with the build up of pressure on the central front, he had asked Giffard for details of his reinforcement programme and on the 6th he left to visit Stilwell on the northern front, receiving a welcome

The Chindits. An airstrip is cleared for Wingate's men to land

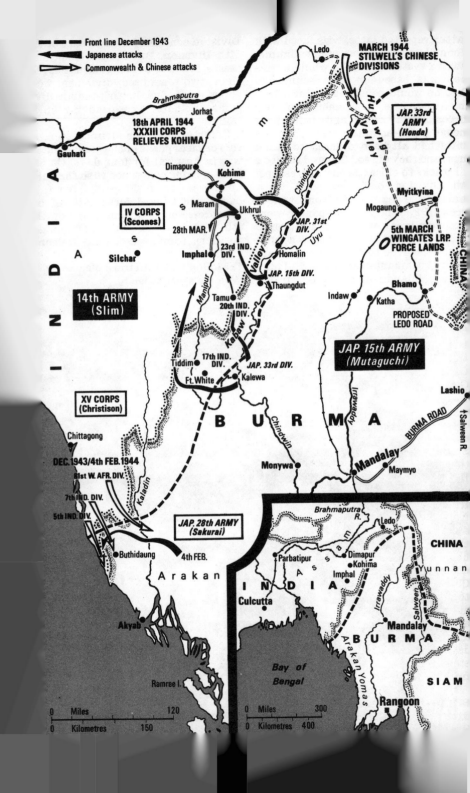

Front line December 1943
Japanese attacks
Commonwealth & Chinese attacks

MARCH 1944
STILWELL'S CHINESE
DIVISIONS

Ledo

Brahmaputra

Jorhat

18th APRIL 1944
XXXIII CORPS
RELIEVES KOHIMA

Hukawng Valley

JAP. 33rd
ARMY
(Honda)

Gauhati

Dimapur

Kohima

Chindwin

Myitkyina

Mogaung

CHINA

IV CORPS
(Scoones)

Maram

Ukhrul

28th MAR.

JAP. 31st
DIV.

Uyu

5th MARCH
WINGATE'S LRP.
FORCE LANDS

Silchar

Imphal

23rd IND.
DIV.

Homalin

JAP. 15th DIV.

Bhamo

Indaw

Katha

14th ARMY
(Slim)

Tamu

Thaungdut

20th IND.
DIV.

PROPOSED
LEDO ROAD

Kabaw Valley

Manipur

Tiddim

17th IND.
DIV.

Ft. White

Kalewa

JAP. 33rd DIV.

JAP. 15th ARMY
(Mutaguchi)

Lashio

Irrawaddy

XV CORPS
(Christison)

B U R M A

Chindwin

BURMA ROAD

↑Salween R.

Chittagong

Monywa

Mandalay

Maymyo

DEC. 1943/4th FEB. 1944

81st W. AFR. DIV.

Kaladin

7th IND. DIV.

5th IND. DIV.

JAP. 28th ARMY
(Sakurai)

Brahmaputra R.

Ledo

CHINA

Buthidaung

4th FEB.

Parbatipur

Dimapur

Kohima

Assam

Imphal

Yunnan

A r a k a n

I N D I A

Culcutta

Irrawaddy

Mandalay

Akyab

Salween

B U R M A

SIAM

Ramree I.

Bay of
Bengal

Arakan Yomas

Rangoon

0   Miles   120
0   Kilometres   150

0   Miles   300
0   Kilometres   400

which was not exactly effusive. Since Stilwell had sent his own mission to Washington in opposition to 'Axiom' relations between the two commanders had cooled considerably. Stilwell wrote of this meeting: 'Louis in at 2.45 . . . Went to headquarters and he made a dumb speech. Then we talked till 4.45. Usual attempt to get me to commit myself.'

Leaving Stilwell's headquarters, Mountbatten was driving a jeep when the main stem of a cut down bamboo sprang up from under the front wheel and struck him with such force as nearly to knock an eyeball out of its socket. He was taken to a nearby American hospital where both eyes were bandaged. He left on the 10th, long before the doctors thought it safe to do so, and long before they thought it advisable to remove the bandages. He immediately flew down to Fourteenth Army and Third Tactical Air Force Headquarters at Comilla, having called a meeting with General Slim and Air Marshal Baldwin. There he was briefed on the full extent of the position and personally decided to fly in the 5th Indian Division immediately; and gave orders to Slim which he said he would confirm to Gifford when he reached him in Delhi later that day.

To move the 5th Indian Division from the Arakan front to the Central front Mountbatten took the risk of diverting thirty Dakota aircraft from the American transport force which had been used for conveying war materials over the Himalayas into China, although he had already been told by the President that he was not authorised to interfere with these aircraft. He reported what he had done, and subsequently, several days after he had taken the necessary steps, received authority for his action from the Chiefs of Staff.

Mountbatten also decided that 2nd British Division should be brought up from central India to defend Kohima. He issued direct orders to Gifford to make the move and asked Auchin-

General Sir Henry Pownall

leck to speed it up. Gifford was not pleased to receive this order as he had told the Divisional Commander only two days earlier that it would not be possible to employ the division in Fourteenth Army area. Gifford still protested that he would not be able to maintain it there, but Mountbatten said he would personally take the risk. Mountbatten also insisted that the whole of XXXIII Indian Corps headquarters, and the Corps Commander General Stopford, should move into the Fourteenth Army area at once.

On 3rd April Mountbatten and Slim paid another visit to Stilwell at Jorhat. Though XXXIII Indian Corps Headquarters had installed itself at Dimapur, to direct operations south towards Imphal, the situation was far from happy. On 28th March the Japanese had cut the Kohima-Imphal road, and now Sato's advance guard was in sight of Kohima itself. There seemed little to stop him breaking through to the Brahmaputra valley and cutting Stilwell's communications. As Mountbatten found, Stilwell was so alarmed at the danger to his communications that he was threatening to postpone

Transport problems in the mud at Imphal

his advance on Myitkyina. Anxious that the pressure on the Japanese 18th Division should not be eased – in case it was diverted to the Imphal front – Slim insisted that he went ahead as planned. When Stilwell asked what he was supposed to do if the Japanese severed his communications in the Brahmaputra valley, Slim gave a guarantee that they would not be interrupted for more than ten days. So the bargain was struck, which soon afterwards Mountbatten approved. According to the entry in his diary, Stilwell seemed somewhat surprised at the coolness of the British commanders at this moment of crisis: 'Conference. Usual slop. Reviewed the situation. Much to my surprise no question of help from us. On contrary, Slim and Supreme Commander said to go ahead.' Though not quite flattering this was rather better than his letter to Mrs Stilwell the previous day: 'Just a line before hopping off to see Louis who, to put it mildly, has his hind leg over his neck. If they don't buck up on their side, we also will have our tit in the ringer. What a mess the Limeys can produce in short order.'

Had Lord Louis got 'his hind leg over his neck?' Not quite – but the generals were certainly continuing to put a strain on him. Stopford, commander XXXIII Corps, in his anxiety to protect Dimapur, had withdrawn the 161st Brigade from Kohima. Slim, realising how hard Kohima would be to retake, now ordered him to send the brigade back. Unfortunately, however, only one battalion got in before the road was closed. But at least there was one saving clause: on 15th March Mountbatten had warned the Chiefs of Staff that the Imphal road would be cut off and that the base would have to be supplied by air for which he would need more aircraft. The Chiefs of Staff agreed with his assessment, but reported that there were no aircraft to

Major-General W D A Lentaigne, who took over the Chindits

send. The only course, they added, was to ask the Americans to extend the loan of twenty Curtiss Commandos and authorise a diversion of seventy Dakotas from the air ferry route. However, the reply from Washington was that although the Commandos could be kept till the end of May, no planes must be transferred from the China ferry. Mountbatten's best hope, they suggested, was to borrow planes from the Middle East. So it was agreed that sixty-four American and twenty-five RAF planes should be allotted – of which in fact a total of seventy-nine flew in. If the ground defences of Imphal held, and if the road from Dimapur could be opened by early May, there was still a chance that the central front could be held, and that the Japanese Fifteenth Army would batter itself to pieces. But at times the chance seemed slim.

In the event, the battles of Imphal and Kohima lasted for three months – and in their ferocity and duration were unique in the history of British-Indian arms. They were soldiers' battles, with small groups of men fighting to the death among the jungle and mountains, often with little knowledge of what was going on to left or to right. At Imphal it was the Japanese who were attacking and the British who were defending, while at Kohima the reverse situation was maintained. Having captured the entire ridge, except for a small central area called Garrison Hill, the Japanese had to be pushed off it yard by yard and inch by inch. Superb diggers, they honeycombed the steep slopes with bunkers, which proved secure against mortars and artillery fire, and to all but a direct hit from the air. Fortunately for the British, it was found possible to cut tracks up the hills for the medium tanks, which then closed with the bunkers and blew them up at pointblank range. Meanwhile the infantry went forward with flamethrowers and grenades, fighting at close quarters, and very often hand to hand. For over a month the two sides

Above: A Chindit patrol in Burma. *Below:* Supplies are loaded for air drop to the Chindits

were separated by the width of the tennis court in the District Commissioner's garden.

To the troops, sweating it out in their weapon pits, the battle seemed formless, but there was an overall pattern, which developed with painful slowness. Thanks to the American and RAF airstrikes, the depredations of Wingate's Chindits, and Mutaguchi's own stupidity, the Japanese supply system was beginning to fail. Their guns ran short of shells, and their mortars of bombs; and the troops were forced to live on a bowl of rice a day. The medical arrangements which had been sketchy to start with began to break down. The tide of war thus began to swing towards the British, although they too had their supply problems, and their bitter setbacks. One of these was the death of Orde Wingate, killed in a plane crash on 25th March. So far his Chindit operation had been a great success – although Mountbatten never quite knew what to make of him nor really understood his ideas – but now he was succeeded by a lethargic Irishman called Lentaigne who sent the Chindits north to help Stilwell. Neither trained nor equipped to act in such a role, they suffered heavy losses, and in due course Mountbatten had to take action to extricate the survivors, whom the merciless Stilwell was driving to destruction. As April turned to May, three basic facts faced Mountbatten: until the battle of Kohima was won, Imphal could not be relieved. And, unless Imphal was relieved by the time the monsoon broke in May, it might be impossible to maintain IV Corps there, despite the loan of American aircraft. In fact Mountbatten's Chief of Staff, Lieutenant-General Sir Henry Pownall, warned him that the whole Corps might have to surrender!

In the second half of April the situation grew particularly tense. With the entire Fourteenth Army fighting for its life, Mountbatten was being pressed by the Americans to expedite the capture of the Mogaung-Myitkyina area in the north, for development as an oilhead and airbase for the China run. The Chiefs of Staff in London were again mumbling about the Sumatra operation, and he had to tell them that no forces whatever were available for this. Giffard was already warning him that the Imphal-Kohima struggle would not be over till the end of May – which was well after the monsoon broke. On 20th April, Slim signalled that the seventy-nine Dakotas on loan from the Middle East would have to remain until 1st July. Without them, IV Corps could not be supplied, and the situation would rapidly deteriorate. On the 25th, passing this information to the Chiefs of Staff, Mountbatten pleaded that the aircraft should stay till the course of battle warranted their removal, only to be warned on the 28th that the middle of May was the absolute limit. Faced with this desperate situation on all sides, Mountbatten signalled again, putting the situation in even plainer language. If he lost these aircraft, he said, the following consequences would ensue: the Chindits would be pulled out, Stilwell's advance would be halted, and at least one division would have to be pulled out of the Imphal Plain. In short, all offensive operations would have to be abandoned, and the Burma front would crumble.

Impatiently Mountbatten awaited a reply to his signal, but by 4th May there was still silence from London. To make matters worse, he was now warned by his own Air Commander-in-Chief, Air Marshal Peirse, that, failing further word from the Chiefs of Staff, the Dakotas must be flown out by the 8th – in four days time. To this Mountbatten retorted that he was the Supremo and not one aircraft would leave the theatre of war without his orders. He personally would take full responsibility for this decision. It was therefore with some relief that the same evening he received a telegram from Winston Churchill: 'Let nothing go from the battle that you need for

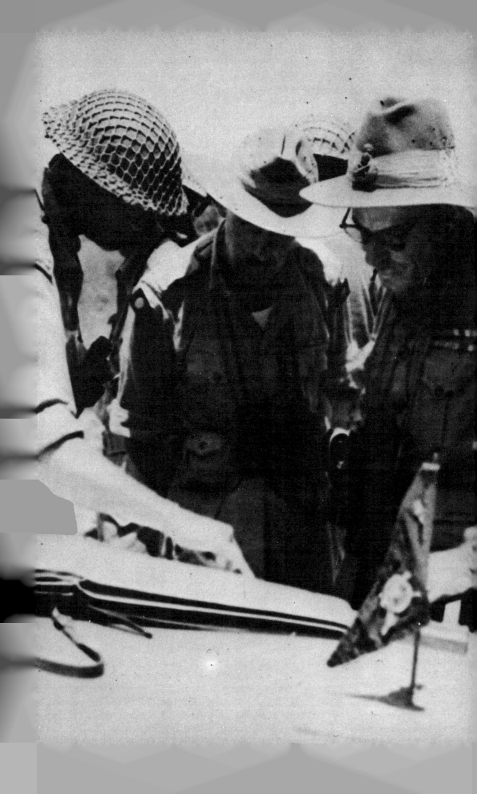

victory. I will not accept denial of this from any quarter, and will back you to the full.'

After this the situation eased, if only a little. The airlift to Imphal continued like clockwork, the Dakotas taking in food, ammunition, equipment, and medical supplies, and bringing out casualties. At Kohima the magnificent American and RAF squadrons gave close fighter and bomber support, and dropped supplies to the brigades high up on the jungle-covered mountains and beyond reach even of the mule columns. And on the ground the men of Mountbatten's multi-racial, and multi-lingual command (British, Americans, Punjabis, Mahrattas, Sikhs, Dogras, Jats, Gurkhas, Assamese, Nagas, Chins, and Kachins) forged themselves into a magnificent team and fought on with superb skill and confidence. Time, they believed, was at last on their side.

They were right. Having sacked two divisional commanders, Yamauchi and Yanagida, Mutaguchi now found Sato threatening to disobey orders. On 13th May, with no supplies reaching his division at Kohima, Sato signalled that he proposed to withdraw. To this Mutaguchi replied: 'Maintain your present position for ten days. Within ten days I shall take Imphal and reward you for your services.' But ten days went by, fourteen days, and Sato signalled: 'Since leaving the Chindwin we have not received one bullet from you, nor a grain of rice,' and when this produced no result threatened to withdraw. When Mutaguchi signalled: 'Retreat and I will courtmartial you' Sato replied: 'Do you what you please. I will bring you down with me.' On 31st May, having sent his now famous signal, 'The tactical ability of Fifteenth Army staff lies below that of cadets', Sato gave orders for the retreat, leaving his second-in-command,

Map conference on the Imphal-Kohima road

Miyazaki, to command the rearguard. By 6th June, as news came through the radios of the landings in Normandy, Kohima ridge was cleared at last and the first great victory was won. It took sixteen more days before Imphal road was open, Miyazaki fighting a series of rearguard actions at Maram, Mao Songsang, and other formidable positions in the mountains. But day after day his men were dying of wounds and starvation, and the armoured column of the 2nd British Division was developing a fine momentum, advancing up to twenty miles in a day. So on 22nd June, with only 400 men left and most of these barely fit for action, Miyazuki turned off the road and headed east for the Chindwin. That afternoon, at milestone 108, Captain Sean Kelly of the Durham Light Infantry realised that the men approaching him were not Japanese but Indians, and soon by their flashes he could see that they belonged to the 5th Division. So the fighting stopped, and there were handshakes and cheers, and Kelly wrote later: 'We sat alone in the sunshine and smoked and ate. The road was open. It was a lovely day.'

It was certainly a bright day for Mountbatten. Imphal was now transformed from a beleaguered fortress into a base for offensive operations. The twin battles had yielded a double triumph. Reports now coming back from the forward troops and from air reconnaissance built up a vivid picture of the plight of Fifteenth Army, which from 8th July was in full retreat across its entire front. It had lost thousands of men in battle, and was losing thousands more as the thinning columns struggled over the mountain tracks, deep in mud from the monsoon rains. Enjoying the freedom of the skies, the SEAC air forces were now hammering the retreating columns whenever the cloud lifted, bombing the Chindwin crossings, the supply depôts, the ammunition dumps. From now on there was to be one driving motive: the offensive.

Burma victory

'It is not difficult to appreciate what the monsoon means to forces on the ground in Burma: it means five months of wretched ·discomfort, five months of heart-breaking difficulties. The only consolation, in fact, was that now the British-Indian forces were sweeping forward and the Japanese were going back.

But advances, especially long advances over difficult terrain, bring their own problems of supply and maintenance. As Slim's divisions streamed over the Chindwin, the line of communications, by ground and air, grew longer every day. And there were still substantial Japanese forces to be brought to battle. In the north, Twenty-eighth Army was being formed under a capable general called Masaki Honda, while Fifteenth Army under its new commander, Katamura, was being reorganised and reinforced, and Twenty-eighth Army clung to its positions in the Arakan. Slim hoped to fight the decisive battle in the

Towards victory in Burma, March 1945

Shwebo-Yeu area between the Chindwin and the Irrawaddy, for here, on the plain, his tank columns could operate with devastating effect, and in clear skies his air superiority could be exploited. But with the battle won, he would have to race to Rangoon, stretching his line of communications to breaking point. So it became clear to Mountbatten that there must also be an amphibious operation against Rangoon, so that supplies could be poured in from the sea. To mount such an operation, however, it would be necessary to capture the port of Akyab and the island of Ramree, to provide airfields on the Arakan coast from which supply aircraft could fly into central Burma, further south on the route of the Fourteenth Army.

At the beginning of August, Mountbatten was due in London for discussions with Churchill and the Chiefs of Staff, but before leaving, was forced into an ugly dispute with Stilwell over what remained of the Chindits. Having been in the field for over four months, living hard and on inadequate rations, they were almost at the end of their tether, and obviously had to be flown out. On 8th July a medical officer reported to Mountbatten that 'all ranks are physically and mentally worn out and have, on average, lost two to three stones in weight. There are few men who have not had attacks of malaria and most have had as many as seven'. On receipt of this information Mountbatten signalled Stilwell, asking for the dates he had in mind for the relief of the Chindits, stating: 'If they are not soon relieved we may both be faced with the possible serious accusation of keeping men in battle who are unable to defend themselves.' To this Stilwell retorted that he had never objected to the removal of sick men; but he still wanted all the fit men to be kept in action. His attitude to the American troops of Merrill's Marauders was just as uncompromising, and as Mountbatten came to realise, he was completely out of touch with the realities of the situa-

tion. Even fresh troops could not accomplish what he was shrilly demanding of these sick and exhausted men. By the time the Chindits were brought out of action a few weeks later, they had lost 3,628 officers and men in killed, wounded, and missing – almost one-fifth of their total strength.

It may be noted here that with Kamaing and Mogaung captured in June, the latter by Mike Calvert and his Chindits, and Myitkyina on 1st August, Stilwell had gained all three of his objectives. As soon as the monsoon abated, it would be possible for the Ledo road and the pipelines to be driven through, and work to commence on the air staging base. After all the argument and confusion in the north, at long last there was solid success to report. It was Stilwell's last.

On 4th August, Mountbatten arrived in London. His prestige in the nine months he had been away had risen enormously; he was the archi-

tect of the greatest land victory over the Japanese in their entire history. And his men were now poised for even greater victories.

Even so the greeting by the Chiefs of Staff was frosty. The more they thought of the long land advance through Burma the less they liked it, and the more they saw the advantages of an amphibious operation against Rangoon. On the other hand (somewhat illogically) they were insistent that Fourteenth Army maintained the initiative, giving the Japanese no time to recover. After some discussion it was clear that the Chiefs of Staff wanted the amphibious operation 'Dracula' to constitute the main thrust, the overland advance 'Capital' being subservient. This view, quite naturally, led to friction with the Americans, who still wanted the China road opened as soon as possible. In the event, the resources for

Mule train, a vital link in the Burma supply train

Above: A tank of 5th Indian Division on route for Tiddim. *Below:* Stillwell, Merrill and fellow officers at the newly captured Myitkyin airfield

Above: Merrill's Marauders out on patrol in Northern Burma. *Below:* Michael Calvert and fellow Chindits after an action

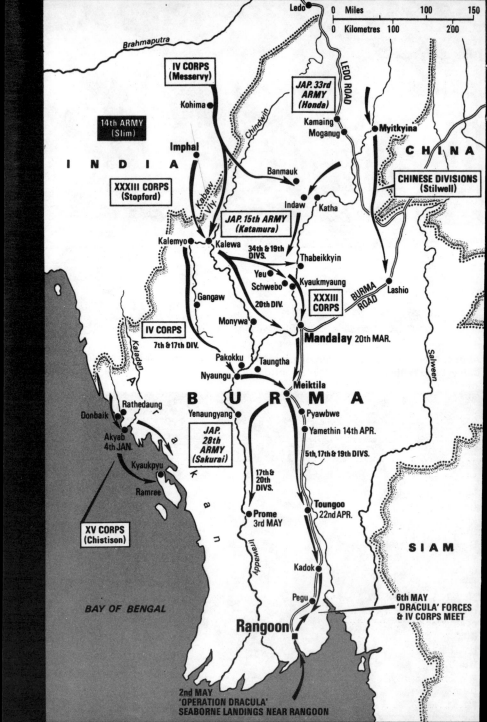

'Dracula' could not be found, so 'Capital' had to be accepted. Fortunately for Mountbatten, working on the previous directive, Giffard and Slim had pressed ahead with the overland advance with all speed. But some indication of Mountbatten's dilemma, through the vacillation of the Chiefs of Staff, can be gauged from a signal he sent Giffard in August from the Chiefs of Staff office in London as a result of directions given to him at that morning's meeting with the Chiefs of Staff. This demanded that, to prevent the involvement in 'Capital' of troops required for 'Dracula', the pursuit of the Japanese should be halted. Fortunately, Stilwell (sitting in as Deputy Commander SEAC) together with Giffard and Slim, protested that such a course was madness – and the pursuit went on. Eventually the Chiefs of Staff became reconciled to the land victory which Fourteenth Army was now offering them.

In the autumn there came some important changes in the command structure of SEAC. Since July, Mountbatten had been agitating to get rid of Giffard and Eleventh Army Group Headquarters, anxious to appoint one man to deal with all three fronts in Burma. Initially, the Americans would not agree, but in October 1944, when Chiang Kai-shek demanded the recall of Stilwell, in whom he had lost confidence, Mountbatten pressed the matter again. So ALFSEA came into existence – Allied Land Forces South-East Asia–and its commander was to be General Sir Oliver Leese, a Guardsman who had previously commanded the Eighth Army. It was November when he arrived, ignorant of the Far East and of the problems of dealing with large forces in such a difficult terrain. Slim can hardly have welcomed the change, having worked so amicably with Giffard whom he greatly admired. And Leese himself did not help matters by sacking many experienced officers at Eleventh Army Group and replacing

General Sir Oliver Leese

them by newcomers from the Middle East. These changes, it may be added, took place while the Fourteenth Army was in full pursuit of the enemy.

By early December Slim realised that the Japanese had no intention of giving battle in the Shwebo-Yeu area. This meant that he would have to pursue them over the Irrawaddy, and therefore, a new plan would be called for. This he now called 'Extended Capital'. Because of the lack of communications he could not bypass Mandalay, but would have to take it together with the ancient fort erected there by the kings of Burma, before heading south. In other words, the long trek which Churchill, Mountbatten and the Chiefs of Staff had dreaded for so long, would now take place. There was no alternative.

When Mountbatten saw Slim's plan, however, he saw immediately that it was brilliant. XXXIII Corps would secure a bridgehead over the Irrawaddy, to the north of Mandalay. Believing this to be the main offensive, Kimura would shift his reserves north accordingly. Meanwhile IV Corps would swing from the left

Defensive positions on the banks of the Irrawaddy

flank of Fourteenth Army to the right, then seize a bridgehead on the Irrawaddy near Pakokku, some seventy miles south-west of Mandalay. It would then strike south-east with its mechanised columns for Meiktila. This was the key point on the Japanese rail and road communications, and once it was taken Fifteenth and Twenty-third Armies would be cut off from their bases in the south. Kimura would find himself checkmated. Plotted in detail by Slim's staff, the plan worked beautifully in execution, and indeed is rated by some historians as the most superbly delivered coup of the entire war. The timing was as follows. On 14th January the 19th Division (of XXXIII Corps) struck to the north of Mandalay at Thabeikkyin, and Kyaukymyaung. On 12th February the 20th Division attacked to the west of Mandalay, where the river describes a large curve. Then from 13th February 7th and 17th Divisions of IV Corps struck at the Pakokku sector

Fourteenth Army troops move up through Pyawbwe, April 1945

to the south. Mazaki Honda, Commander Twenty-third Army, whichhad now retreated so far south that the Ledo road was open, has recounted how Kimura's Chief of Staff, Tanaka, held a conference at Meiktila to discuss Slim's offensive. Honda and Katamura argued that he would make a powerful thrust towards the base where they were now meeting, but Tanaka disagreed. While the argument was still in progress, a signal arrived giving the news that a column 'of 200 vehicles' was approaching. In due course it was learned that the signal was corrupt – the figure should have read '2,000'. Cowan's 17th Division and the 255th Tank Brigade were coming on at speed. By 1st March Cowan had taken Meiktila and the trap was sprung.

There is no need to follow the events which followed in great detail. With Fifteenth Army fragmenting, Kimura ordered Honda to take charge of all operations in the Meiktila area. But when he arrived on 17th March, it was to find Slim's armour and infantry dominating the situation, and the sky full of American and

General D T Cowan, commanding 17th Division, plans the attack on Meiktila

A motorised column advances on Meiktila

British planes. By 29th March Honda knew the battle was lost, and pulled back his battered formations to the south and east.

Now Slim urged on his columns with all speed, 5th, 17th and 19th Divisions in the railway corridor on the east flank, and 7th and 20th in the Irrawaddy Valley on the west. The key battle was fought at Pyawbwe on 10th April, where with great dash, Cowan's men slaughtered 2,000 Japanese – the entire garrison. The race for Rangoon was on.

By the end of December SEAC naval forces had retained control of the Bay of Bengal, and the Royal Navy was roving as far east as Sumatra. To Mountbatten's delight amphibious operations were possible once more, and plans were put in hand for retaking Akyab, and assaulting Ramree Island. The latter operation was mounted from Chittagong on 21st January, 1945, the armada including the battleship *Queen Elizabeth*, the cruiser *Phoebe*, the destroyers *Rapid*

Supplies are unloaded at Ramree Island

and *Napier*, and other minor vessels, with air cover provided by 224 Group RAF and eighty-five Liberators of the Strategic Air Force. Though some of the landing craft struck mines, the landing was unopposed. It was over a week before the Japanese mobilised their forces and then there was heavy fighting at the exits of Kyaukpyu, the only town in the island. By this time the tanks were ashore, and gradually the Japanese forces found their escape routes to the mainland being cut by the navy. Those who were not shot were drowned in the swamps; and hundreds hid themselves in the jungle till the war was over. Now work went rapidly ahead to prepare Ramree as an airfield to enable the leading elements of the Fourteenth Army to be supplied by air from the Arakan coast. Ramree was also prepared as a base for Operation Dracula if it should be required for this purpose.

With the Japanese fighting just as ferociously as ever whenever a defensive position presented itself, Slim feared they would try to make a last stand in the streets of Rangoon.

Landing craft move up Rangoon river following an air strike

Troops disembark at Rangoon. There was little resistance

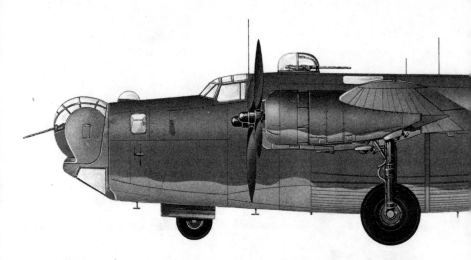

Consolidated PB4Y-1 (based on the B-24D Liberator) *Engines:* four Pratt & Whitney R-1830 radials, 1,200hp each at 25,000 feet. *Armament:* eight .5-inch Browning machine guns with 3,770 rounds and up to 8,000lbs of bombs. *Speed:* 287mph at 26,700 feet. *Climb:* 990 feet per minute initially. *Ceiling:* 32,600 feet. *Range:* 2,065 miles with full bomb load. *Weight empty/loaded:* 37,160/63,000lbs. *Span:* 110 feet. *Length:* 67 feet 3 inches.

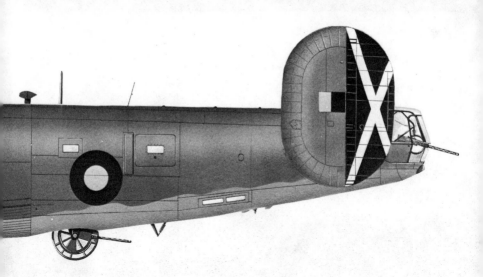

Here, it was imagined they had food-stocks and ammunition to last weeks, and by fighting from street to street and house to house, could hold up Fourteenth Army until its long and now seriously overstretched line of communications had snapped. So Slim approached Mountbatten with a plea that 'Dracula' should be re-considered, and on 2nd April Mountbatten – delighted yet again that the Royal Navy could be brought into play – ordered an assault by one division, with a drop by a battalion of parachute troops. The operation, Mountbatten ordered, should take place not later than 5th May.

In fact the navy decided that 2nd May was the latest date the weather would allow, and between 27th and 30th April six convoys sailed from Akyab and Ramree, covered by a large force of fighter aircraft, and escorted by a naval force of two battleships (one British and one French), two escort carriers, three cruisers, and six destroyers. On 1st May a heavy bombing attack was launched against defences on the Rangoon River, followed by the dropping of parachute troops on Elephant

Point. There was very little resistance, and a plane circling over Rangoon saw written in large letters on the jail roof, 'Japs gone. Exdigitate.' This, as Slim, remarked, was a gentle hint to speed up operations. So, on 3rd May, Slim's men, completing their long overland journey from the north, linked up with the seaborne troops from the south; and Rangoon was free again.

But the fighting in Burma was not over yet. With Fourteenth Army cutting the country in two like a giant sword, the troops of Sakurai's Twenty-eighth Army found themselves trapped in the Arakan and, aided by a diversion from the remnants of Honda's army, were soon making frantic efforts to get out. Thousands were killed as they left the jungles, thousands were drowned in the rivers or lost in the swamps. As May wore on the parties trying to cross grew smaller, and eventually ceased altogether. There were no more to come. Sakurai's army had been destroyed just as surely as Honda's and Katamura's. 190,000 men lay dead on the fields – the greatest number counted in any campaign in the Far East. The Allied victory was devastating and complete.

Rangoon receives the Allies

East to Malaya

For Mountbatten the final victory in Burma posed new and in some ways even more serious problems. Malaya, Singapore, Siam (Thailand), and Sumatra, all remained in Japanese hands and would have to be re-taken. Combined Operations on a great scale and over vast distances would be called for. And with the war in Europe over at last, there was the promise of more ships, more landing craft, and more men. Planning for these new operations had already begun when he discovered that his subordinates were arranging to leave Slim in Burma with a small occupation force, called Twelfth Army, while Fourteenth Army, under a new commander, would be withdrawn from Burma and prepare for the Malayan invasion. By now, of course, Slim's prestige was enormous, and his hold over the troops was complete. It was inconceivable that he should be robbed of his command. So Stopford was left in Burma,

Leese went home, and Slim replaced him at ALFSEA.

But in June, as the monsoon arrived, and Mountbatten held a victory parade in Rangoon, the Secretary of State for War suddenly announced that demobilisation was to be speeded up, and that all men with three years four months service were to be sent home as soon as possible without awaiting replacement. So again plans had to be scaled down.

As well as grappling with forward plans and manpower problems, Mountbatten now took over a third task: responsibility for the government and welfare of fourteen million Burmese. This in some ways was the most difficult problem of all, presenting him with a challenge for which his experience could provide no guide. When the British had evacuated Burma in 1942, the Governor, Sir Reginald Dorman-Smith, had set up a government-in-exile, and confidently expected to return to Rangoon once the military victory had been won.

Japan in defeat: a sword surrendered

But, in Mountbatten's phrase, Burmese nationalism now emerged as a force to reckon with.' The Commander-in-Chief of the Burma National Army, Major-General Aung San, could no longer be ignored; the BNA was now the only body with wide popular backing. To complicate matters, after fighting with the Japanese until March 1945, Aung San had then switched sides and helped the British. To Dorman-Smith and the pre-1942 Establishment in Burma, he was a traitor who deserved to be shot. But Mountbatten realised the importance of retaining the goodwill of the Burmese people, and in June he issued the following directive: 'The guiding principle which I am determined shall be observed is that no person shall suffer on account of political opinions honestly held, whether now or in the past, even if these may have been anti-British, but only on account of proven crimes against the criminal law, or actions repugnant to humanity. The principle is no more than an elementary point of British justice.'

This – to many people radical – viewpoint was misunderstood both by the majority of the Civil Affairs officers no less than by Aung San and his supporters. Thirsting for executive power, the latter now asked to have Civil Government brought back into Rangoon, and Mountbatten agreed, so making, as he confessed later, a grave mistake. If the move had been delayed, there would have been a chance at least of Burma remaining in the British Commonwealth. Instead, after the new Burmese Nationalist Government got at loggerheads with the civil Governor, she decided to leave, and today,

Left: **Major-General Aung San, later assassinated.** *Below:* **Victory Day parade in Rangoon**

isolated and increasingly xenophobic, has been bypassed by the main stream of world affairs and still grapples with grave internal problems.

Mountbatten's decision was not taken on his initiative alone, as is sometimes suggested. On 12th December 1944 the Secretary of State for Burma had stated in the House of Commons that Burma would be given self-government as soon as possible. Mountbatten merely gave this policy a very liberal interpretation.

By mid-July, having handed over Burma and its problems to the Civil Government, Mountbatten bent his mind to the strategic problems now facing him. With 'Zipper', the invasion of Malaya, in the advanced planning stage, he thought it high time to co-ordinate plans with General MacArthur, the Supreme Commander in the South-West Pacific. On 10th July at Manila they met for the first time, Mountbatten recording later, 'He was a terrific man. His methods were quite unlike mine; he was absolutely autocratic; he never really consulted his Army, Air or Fleet Commanders. He made up his own mind and told them what to do.' At this meeting it was agreed that SEAC squadrons would assist in the air offensive against Borneo and Java, and against Japanese shipping.

From Manila Mountbatten flew to the last of the great inter-Allied war conferences at Potsdam. Here it was decided that operational strategy in the Pacific should remain in the hands of the American Chiefs of Staff, while control of a large part of the South-West Pacific Area should be transferred immediately after the Japanese surrender to Mountbatten, who still

Left: **Mountbatten and McArthur.**
Below: **Mountbatten arrives for the Potsdam conference**

SEAC commanders draw up surrender terms, August 1945

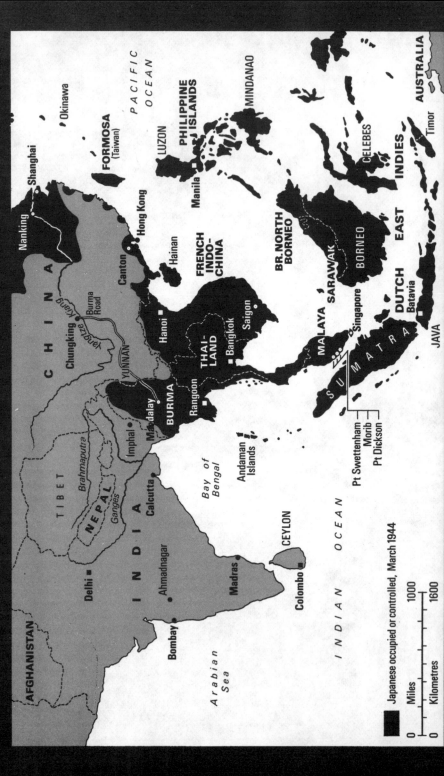

PACIFIC OCEAN

Okinawa

Shanghai

Nanking

FORMOSA
(Taiwan)

PHILIPPINE
ISLANDS

LUZON

MINDANAO

Hong Kong

Canton

Hainan

Manila

CHINA

FRENCH
INDO-
CHINA

CELEBES

EAST
INDIES

Timor

AUSTRALIA

Chungking

Burma Road

Yangtze Kiang

Hanoi

BR. NORTH
BORNEO

BORNEO

SARAWAK

YUNNAN

THAI-
LAND

Bangkok

Saigon

MALAYA

DUTCH

Batavia

Mandalay

BURMA

Rangoon

Singapore

SUMATRA

JAVA

Imphal

Brahmaputra

TIBET

NEPAL

Ganges

Calcutta

Bay of
Bengal

Andaman
Islands

Pt Swettenham
Morib
Pt Dickson

Delhi

INDIA

Ahmadnagar

Madras

CEYLON

AFGHANISTAN

Bombay

Arabian
Sea

Colombo

INDIAN OCEAN

■ Japanese occupied or controlled, March 1944

Miles   0   1000

Kilometres   0   1600

had responsibilities to the Americans, though of course through the British Chiefs of Staff. Soon after Potsdam, on 20th July, the Combined Chiefs of Staff gave Mountbatten a new directive, by which his tasks were laid down as follows: the liberation of Malaya, the capture of key areas of Siam, and the maintenance of pressure on the Burma-Siam frontier. He was also ordered to establish bridgeheads in Java or Sumatra. And Singapore, once back in British hands, would be developed as a base for operations towards the Japanese mainland.

But the first and most important operation was 'Zipper' – a great Combined Operation of enormous complexity for which plans had been agreed on 25th June. Almost 250,000 troops would take part, embarking at Bombay, Colombo, Madras, Calcutta, and Rangoon. Steaming on an agreed time schedule, the invasion fleets would come together in the Indian Ocean, and head east towards their objectives, with massive naval and air cover. This was by far the biggest Combined Operation ever undertaken in the Far East, the only comparable operation being the cross-Channel invasion on Normandy. But in 'Zipper' the distances could be measured not in tens of miles but in hundreds; the troops from Bombay had to steam for well over 2,000 miles; and would be at sea over a week. D-Day was finally fixed for 9th September.

Watching the organisation going ahead with such professionalism – the smooth concentration of transports, landing craft, landing ships, battleships, aircraft carriers, together with some 17,000 vehicles, 2,250 animals, and 225,000 tons of stores and petrol, Mountbatten would normally have experienced a great sense of pride and achievement. Before his work at Combined Operations headquarters, such an operation would have been quite impossible; the techniques had not been evolved, and the specialised craft and equipment had neither been manufactured nor even designed. Brought to a successful conclusion, 'Zipper' would have been a great and glorious end to his career as Supreme Commander. But, in fact, as he knew, 'Zipper' would not take place as an operation of war; and the landings on Singapore island and the Malayan coast, would be unopposed. At Potsdam he had heard for the first time of the development of the atomic bomb, which was about to be dropped on Japan. According to the American Chiefs of Staff, Japan would have surrendered by mid-August.

Here then was the extraordinary situation in which Mountbatten found himself. Churchill's orders were, 'You must tell your Staff to prepare to sail the Zipper invasion fleet as early as possible on the definite assumption that there would be no opposition to the landing of the troops – but without giving any explanation.' To this Mountbatten retorted that his staff would think him mad, to which Churchill replied that his staff must not question his sanity but must obey his orders.

It was the 6th August before the SEAC planners realised what Mountbatten was talking about, for on this date the first atom bomb was dropped on Hiroshima. After stalling and arguing the Japanese war leaders agreed to the surrender terms on 14th August. And a week later 'Zipper' went ahead.

On 12th September came the surrender ceremony at Singapore Town Hall, a ceremony which Mountbatten was determined should remain in the memory of all who saw it for life. For the troops it was to be the real taste of victory, the seal on their achievements over the past two years. Holding this view, Mountbatten disagreed profoundly with General MacArthur, who had laid down strict orders that Japanese officers should not give up their *samurai* swords, because they would lose face and therefore control over their men. Later he wrote: 'I was determined that they *should* lose face. So I insisted on senior

Japanese officers surrender to 25th Indian Division

Mountbatten arrives in Singapore for the surrender ceremony

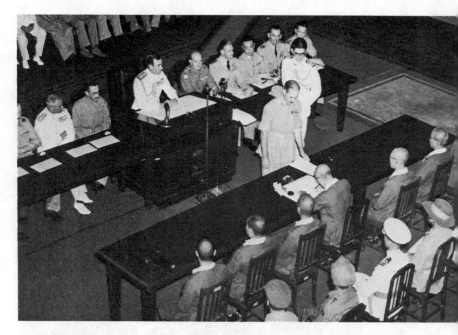

General Itagaki signs the surrender document

Three cheers for the King

Field-Marshal Count Hisaichi Terauchi

General Seishiro Itagaki

137

commander's' swords being handed over in Singapore, and in all other appropriate places under my command. I don't think there was any doubt in the minds of those who witnessed the Japanese surrenders whether the Japanese were beaten or not.'

With this concept in mind, the ceremony was stage-managed. In the ante-chamber stood a token force of Chinese troops with their British officers, grouped round the eight main pillars, each pillar representing one of the Allied nations. A British airman stood at the door to the Chamber, inside which were arranged two long tables, one for the Allied delegates and one for the Japanese. In the centre of the first table was a raised dais for Mountbatten himself.

On his journey to the Town Hall Mountbatten travelled in an open car with his American Deputy Supreme Allied Commander, General R A Wheeler, through streets lined with sailors and Royal Marines. At the Municipal Buildings he was received by his three Allied Commanders-in-Chief and all the high ranking Allied officers in Singapore. Having inspected four guards of honour, while the massed bands of the fleet played 'Rule Britannia', he paused while the Royal Artillery fired a salute of seventeen guns. Then, immaculate in his white naval uniform, he led the galaxy of commanders into the building. Here, 400 spectators had been given seats, many of whom were released prisoners of war; there were photographers and teams of camera men; and the galleries were crowded with representatives of the press. The Japanese delegates were then ushered in: General Itagaki of Seventh Area Army, General Kimura of Nakamura of Eighteenth Area Army, Lieutenant-General Kinoshita of Third Air Army, Vice-Admiral Shibata of Second Southern Expeditionary Fleet and

Terauchi hands over his own sword to Mountbatten

three others. Each delegate was accompanied by an armed escort of appropriate rank. At a signal the whole assembly rose and, followed by four ADCs, Mountbatten entered the room and moved majestically to the dais. The strained silence was broken as he read a prepared statement: 'I have come here today to receive the formal surrender of all the Japanese forces within South-East Asia Command . . .

'In addition to our Naval, Military and Air forces which we have present in Singapore today, a large fleet is anchored off Port Swettenham and Port Dickson, and a large force started disembarking from them at daylight on 9th September. When I visited the beaches yesterday, men were landing in an endless stream. As I speak there are 100,000 men ashore. This invasion would have taken place on 9th September whether the Japanese had resisted or not. I wish to make this plain; the surrender today is no negotiated surrender. The Japanese are submitting to superior forces, now massed here.'

In his absence, Field-Marshal Count Terauchi, who had just suffered a heart attack, had sent a written authorisation for General Itagaki to act on his behalf. Mountbatten now called on the general to produce his credentials, and read them and the Instrument of Surrender to the assembled company. Then the two commanders each signed eleven copies of the Instrument of Surrender, one each for the Allied nations, one for King George VI, one for the Japanese Government, one for Mountbatten personally, and one for SEAC records. Leaving the Chamber, Mountbatten and his entourage took up their position on the terrace before the Municipal Buildings, and after his Order of the Day had been read, a Union Jack which had been concealed in Changi Jail since the surrender of 1942 was broken from the masthead while the massed bands played the National Anthems of the Allied nations.

o Whitehall
Via Delhi

At the end of the surrender ceremony n Singapore I ceased to be a fighting ommander. The problems I had to eal with now were political and uman problems on a terrifying scale.' Iountbatten did not exaggerate the tate of affairs in the territories now urrendered by Japan, nor the extent f his own responsibilities. Apart rom Burma, Malaya, Singapore, Siam nd Sumatra, he now was responsible or the rest of the Dutch East Indies nd French Indo-China up to the ixteenth Parallel. Later on, Borneo nd Dutch New Guinea were temporrily added to the list. The population f these areas totalled 128 million eople, many of them living amidst evastation and large numbers faced vith starvation.

Not unnaturally, the peoples of sia detested the presence of the apanese prisoners of war, over 750,000 f them, and efforts had to be made to epatriate them, despite the shortage

of shipping. While they waited for ships, the prisoners were set to work cleaning up the towns, repairing buildings, and restoring sanitation. Outside the towns, peace had not yet returned: local populations had formed resistance groups and bands of guerillas, and were now prepared to use their weapons to prevent the return of colonial rule, whether British, French, or Dutch.

Yet another problem was presented by the 123,000 Allied prisoners of war, held in some 250 camps throughout the territories. These camps, many deep in the jungle, had firstly to be located, and then provided with food and medical supplies before the prisoners, thousands of whom were near death, could be rescued. Lady Mountbatten, who had flown out at her husband's request to help with the repatriation of prisoners of war, later reported to the Red Cross: 'There is no doubt that had the war gone on a few more weeks there would have been no prisoners of war in these areas left alive at all. They were absolutely at their last gasp.'

In Singapore there was trouble from the Chinese Communist Party, who with the departure of the Japanese, now concentrated its efforts on expelling the British. In January and February 1946 it tried to bring down the administration by a series of strikes and mass demonstrations, and Mountbatten's advisers urged that if necessary the ring leaders should be arrested and shot. But Mountbatten refused. Though severely criticised for his attitude, he believed that the rising tide of nationalism in Asia should not be fought. The era of colonialism was coming to an end, and the sooner the fact was recognised the better.

This attitude presented many difficulties, especially over the French and Dutch territories which Britain was pledged to hand back to her Allies. These powers had not the resources to take over immediately themselves, and so in the resultant power vacuum, Communists and extreme nationalists flourished. In French Indo-China, covering the states now known as Laos, Cambodia, and Vietnam, the weak French forces tried to assert themselves, but came up against the nationalist leader, Ho Chi-Minh, who, while in exile in China five years earlier, had set up a League for the Independence of Vietnam. Though a Communist, Ho Chi-Minh received American backing as an anti-colonialist. Not for the first time, through their obsession over colonialism, the Americans were sowing dragons' teeth. The British, of course, were obliged to support the French, and so there came about a split in Anglo-American policy which prevented any satisfactory settlement of the problem. At the same time Ho Chi-Minh's power grew as a result of Chiang Kai-shek's failure to compete with him north of the Sixteenth Parallel, where Chiang took over responsibility for post-surrender tasks from Mountbatten. Thus there arose the division into North and Sou[th] Vietnam which led to the Vietna[m] War.

The situation was little better [in] Indonesia, where, two days befo[re] their surrender, the Japanese ha[d] warned Dr Achmed Sukarno, t[he] nationalist leader, of their intention[.] Taking his chance, Sukarno set up [a] Central Advisory Council to prepa[re] for independence, his forces bei[ng] trained by Japanese officers and NCO[s.] On 17th August 1945 he proclaim[ed] Indonesia a republic.

In March 1946 Mountbatten wa[s] submitted to yet another test [of] diplomacy, when Pandit Nehru, [a] member of the Indian Interim Gover[n]ment, arrived for talks with the India[n] community and the Indian troop[s.] The general view amongst Britis[h] officers and administrators in Sing[a]pore was that Nehru should be col[d] shouldered and regarded as hostil[e.] As leader of the Indian Nation[al] Congress Party he had agitated f[or] independence during the most critic[al] phase of the war against Japan, an[d] had consequently been incarcerated i[n] Ahmednagar fort, with many of h[is] lieutenants. Mountbatten, howeve[r,] foresaw that whatever his past recor[d] Nehru was destined to be the fir[st] Prime Minister of India – and even [a] minor discourtesy might have seriou[s] repercussions on future Anglo-India[n] relations. So he held out the hand [of] friendship, which was graspe[d] immediately; and it is not too muc[h] to say that the close relationshi[p] which developed between the tw[o] leaders in Singapore would soon hav[e] a major impact on world history.

In May 1946 Mountbatten's period [of] command came to an end, and h[e] handed over to the Right Honourabl[e] Malcolm MacDonald, who now arrive[d] as Governor-General of Malaya an[d] Singapore and Lord Killearn who wa[s] appointed Special Commissioner fo[r] South-East Asia. By June he wa[s] back in London to play his part in th[e] Victory Parade. Now began to flo[w] the great stream of honours, decora[-]

ove: **Japanese prisoners clean the streets of Singapore.** *Below:* **Lady Louis ountbatten visits released POWs**

Ho Chi-Minh

Doctor Sukarno

Pandit Nehru

Malcolm MacDonald

tions, and awards from Britain and her Allies, which was to continue for some years. King George of England made him a Knight of the Garter, a Privy Councillor, A Knight Grand Commander of the Indian Empire, A Knight Grand Commander of the Star of India, also granted him the title of Earl Mountbatten of Burma. The Americans awarded him their Army Distinguished Service Medal, the Greeks their Military Cross and the Grand Cross of the Order of George I; Chiang Kai-shek awarded him the Special Grand Cordon of the Cloud and Banner; the French the Grand Cross of the Legion of Honour and the Croix de Guerre; the King of Siam the Grand Cross of the Order of the White Elephant; the King of Nepal the Star of Nepal; and the Netherlands Government the Order of the Lion.

His ambition now, however, was to get back to his career in the Royal Navy, in which, shedding his wartime rank, he had now achieved the substantive rank of Rear-Admiral. In due course this ambition would be achieved, but meanwhile there were more political problems to deal with; he was to return to Delhi as the last Viceroy.

Since the Labour Government had come to power in the early summer of 1945, it had been obvious that India would gain her freedom within a few years. The great stumbling block was that the then Viceroy, Lord Wavell, was unable to obtain agreement between the two Indian power-blocks, Nehru's National Congress Party, and Jinnah's Muslim League. To the British, the idea of splitting up the Indian sub-continent, for whose unification they had worked and fought for over a century, was a tragedy too great to be contemplated. And yet increasingly it was becoming obvious that the Muslims wanted Pakistan, their own country, and would not co operate in a Hindu government, whatever concessions were made. Wavell's dogged efforts to be fair led to suspicions on the Congress side that

Above: Indian leaders discuss the plan for partition at the New Delhi conference
Right: Rioting followed partition

he was pro-Muslim – as were the vast majority of British officers – and he was recalled; the man chosen to cut the Gordian knot was Mountbatten.

Not unexpectedly, Mountbatten got on well with Nehru and even with Gandhi, but completely failed to understand – and possibly underrated – Ali Jinnah, the Muslim leader. But he was convinced that June 1948, the suggested date for independence, was too far ahead. With so many months at their disposal, he believed, the Indian leaders would indulge their talents for hair-splitting and the communal massacres which had started in August 1946 and had continued with reprisal massacres would become more frequent and the situation more hopeless than ever. So on 4th June 1947, at an audience of some 300 representatives of the Indian and world press in the Legislative Assembly, he gave a strong hint that the date was being brought forward to 15th August that year. In other words the Indians had a bare two and a half months to agree to his plan

for the dismemberment of the sub-continent, and for the splitting up of the Indian Army, and to come to terms with the Indian princes, who had enjoyed a large measure of independence under the British *raj*. Mountbatten explained the advance of the date as follows: 'The August deadline was really dictated to me by my whole experience since I arrived in India, and above all by the virtual breakdown of normal government.' The explanation seems reasonable enough. Certainly the grim realisation that soon there would be no one to blame for their troubles but themselves sharpened the wits of the Indian politicians. The boundaries of Pakistan were drawn. The Indian Army prepared itself to have its formations, battalions, and even companies split according to religion. And the princes were cajoled into submission; So in August India and Pakistan became sovereign states, and, to their eternal discredit, butchered vast numbers of their own people in the process. The exact numbers will never be known, though the most reliable estimates are 200,000 to 250,000. And in addition 14,000,000 people migrated from their homes to the opposite Dominion and many thousands of young girls were kidnapped by both sides, forcibly converted or sold by auction.

Mountbatten was now fully committed to the role of Governor-General of the new India. The post had been offered to him by Nehru and Patel, and approved by Jinnah, the future Governor-General of Pakistan. So far as India was concerned, the appointment was fortunate, for the communal disturbances were so great during the first three months of the country's independent existence that the state almost fragmented. By forming an Emergency Committee and guiding this closely from day to day, Mountbatten managed to sur-

The Viceroy visits the Frontier Province during the riots

mount the crisis, but all his powers were needed both as a commander and a diplomat. His decision to serve the new India – so taking what might have been judged to constitute a partisan role – was certainly justified.

There was a further crisis on 30th January 1948 when Gandhi was murdered in the grounds of Birla House, Delhi. Hearing the news, Mountbatten hurried to the house and heard a voice in the crowd shouting out, 'It was a Muslim who killed him! A Muslim!' Rounding on the man in a flash, Mountbatten called, 'You fool, don't you know it was a Hindu'. At this stage, he had no idea who the assassin might be; but he realised that if word got round that a Muslim was responsible, there would be civil war. Fortunately the assassin was a Hindu.

In June 1948 Mountbatten handed over to C Rajagopalachari, and came back to England. 'I loved India', he wrote, 'and did my best to serve the people.' To what extent he had succeeded, and to what extent he bears responsibility for the heritage of suspicion and hatred on the sub-continent, may still be argued. But given the extraordinary situation to be resolved, it is difficult to imagine anyone who could have done the job better. At the farewell banquet, Pandit Nehru paid him a most moving tribute: 'You came here, Sir, with a high reputation, but many a reputation has foundered in India. You lived here during a period of great difficulty and crisis, and yet your reputation has not foundered. That is a remarkable feat. Many of us who came into contact with you from day to day in these days of crisis learned much from you. We gathered confidence when sometimes we were rather shaken, and I have no doubt that the many lessons we have learned from you will endure, and will help us in our work in the future.'

This was the last public tribute Mountbatten was to enjoy for some time. Arriving in London, he found the press and Conservative Party

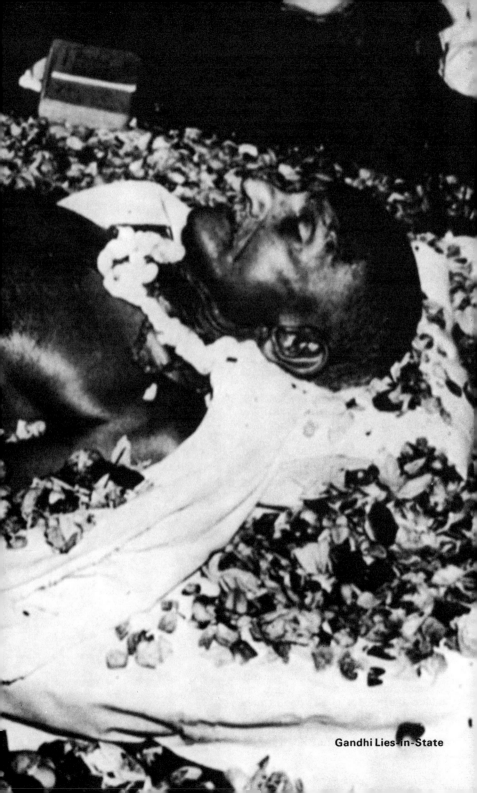

Gandhi Lies-in-State

blaming him for the disorders following partition and independence. He has recorded that old friends turned against him and many people cut him dead. Even Winston Churchill refused to speak to him for his great 'crime' of giving away India. It was therefore fortunate that he had extracted a promise from the Prime Minister, Clement Attlee, that he should be allowed to return to the Royal Navy and in October 1948 he went back to the Mediterranean to command the 1st Cruiser Squadron, with the rank of Rear-Admiral. On the island of Malta, at his base, he recorded with some amusement that he was 'thirteenth in the order of social precedence' and had to take orders from Admirals who had served on his staff or under him when he was Supreme Commander SEAC. Curiously enough, when he had been appointed Chief of Combined Operations in 1942, with accelerated wartime promotion, the naval historian Commander Kenneth Edwards, had written, 'He has, in effect, been lifted out of his generation, and unless he can revert to the rank of Captain and be given a command at sea his subsequent naval career may be cut unduly short.' Was this prophecy to be fulfilled, despite his enormous prestige, and achievements?

In 1949 Mountbatten did not add to his popularity among the admirals by an incident during manoeuvres. Given command of the Mediterranean Fleet, in opposition to the Home Fleet, he managed to infiltrate a telegraphist into the rival headquarters at Gibraltar, who then radioed the movements of their ships on a portable transmitter. Such an action was regarded as unfair and un-British, but Mountbatten defended himself with the remark that 'You can't always expect the enemy to play the game by Queensberry Rules.' Before the year was out, he was obviously set to climb the ladder again. His next appointment was as Fourth Sea Lord; and in May 1952 he went back to the Mediterranean as Commander-in-Chief. Soon he had

The Admiral on Mediterranean manoeuvres, 1954

The popular commander. *Left:* Mountbatten visits General K D Wolfe at a 20th Air Force Bomber Command. *Above:* Address to the troops. *Below:* At Government House, Singapore

Mountbatten was always close to his troops, from his early days with the commandos. *Above:* to his command in South-East Asia. *Below:* during his Mediterranean command, one step away from First Sea Lord

aken on an additional role as Commander-in-Chief Allied Forces, Mediterranean. He was a Supremo for the second time. When his tour came to an end in December 1954, six admirals, representing the six Allied Commanders-in-Chief under him, formed a crew and rowed him to his flagship.

In 1955 he achieved his life's ambition at last, becoming First Sea Lord. The recommendation came from Winston Churchill, during his very last days in high office, the same man who forty-three years earlier had recommended Mountbatten's father to the same job. Mountbatten was head of the Royal Navy for four years, during which many sweeping changes were made, and the service was re-modelled to meet the changing needs of defence, and to recognise Britain's diminishing role on the world stage. This was not his last job, for in 1959 he was appointed Chief of the Defence Staff, and was responsible for initiating and carrying through the most sweeping reforms that the fighting services of Britain have ever undergone. Instead of three separate Ministries, each dealing with its own service, there was to be one – the Ministry of Defence. As Mountbatten put it, 'I knew I would have a terrific struggle, because I would be up against tradition and vested interest – a formidable combination.' Many senior officers predicted chaos and disaster. With his long advocacy of inter-service co-operation, however, Mountbatten was admirably qualified for the job, and when he was due to retire in 1962, the Prime Minister, Harold Macmillan, persuaded him to stay on until the process of integration had been completed. So it was 1965 before he was out of harness. Even then he retained active responsibilities, with new appointments in 1965 as Life Colonel Commandant of the Royal Marines, and the Colonel of the Life Guards, the latter being the first time in British history that an officer in one service has been given an active appointment in another. His service to the Royal Navy, the nation, the Allied cause, and to NATO had lasted half a century.

As must be clear to anyone reading this narrative, Mountbatten has enjoyed honours, rewards, and promotions on a prodigious scale. For forty years or more success has escorted him like a guardian angel. But the question must still be asked: how does he rank as a war leader? To this the answer is surely that he can be directly compared to no one. He worked successfully with armies, as did Marlborough, but never commanded an army in the field. His presence raised morale, as did Wellington's, but he was no trainer of armies. He had the personal magnetism of Hannibal, but can be credited with no military masterpiece. For him it must be said that he succeeded in doing what other men – commanders of considerable stature – had failed to do. He established Combined Operations Headquarters and got its doctrines accepted by all the fighting services, after Admiral Sir Roger Keyes had failed. He raised the morale of the troops in South-East Asia – a task which no one else knew how to begin to tackle. And he succeeded in bringing about the permanent unification of service command and administration in a way that had never been done before. Apart from this, he won the trust of men of all types and races. He got on with Eisenhower as well as with Nehru. He could talk effectively to the Combined Chiefs of Staff – and to his British, Gurkha, and Indian troops.

But perhaps the qualities which lie at the back of Mountbatten's achievements are his physical courage, his energy and his mastery of technology. It was the latter which brought him to prominence, first as Fleet Wireless Officer, and then as Chief of Combined Operations. It was his courage which made him outstanding as a destroyer commander. His decision not to desert the survivors of the *Kashmir*, after both she

and the *Kelly* had been sunk, was superb. Had he done nothing else in the entire war, this would have stamped him as a leader of great quality. His energy, both in war and peace, has been little short of miraculous. Men who served both Churchill and Mountbatten have testified without hesitation that Mountbatten was the harder taskmaster. Asking permission to go home after Indian Independence, Lord Ismay, wrote, 'Six months with you have exhausted me far more than six years doing the same job for Winston.' Once presented a challenge, Mountbatten has always shown little concern for time, food, sleep, or comfort. In this respect, like many great men, he is somewhat inhuman. But it is his vast energies which have allowed him to work at each problem presenting itself, until a solution has been found.

Without denying his achievements, it is hard not to conclude that he has had luck on his side, to quite an extraordinary degree. He was born into a royal house and with a superb physique. Three times when disaster struck the *Kelly* he escaped death or even wounds. And in Burma, perhaps, he was luckiest of all.

As more documents become available and more generals and statesmen pass from the scene, the reputations of all great war leaders will be assessed and re-assessed. What the final verdict on Mountbatten will be it is impossible to say, for the vast majority of documents will not become available until after his death; and for a man living over half his years under a blaze of publicity, he has shown a remarkable flair for reticence. But there can be no doubt, I think, of his essential integrity, his honesty, his courage, and his patriotism. He became a war leader because the Allied cause demanded the use of his extraordinary array of talents. Without him the road to victory would have been harder and longer, and the sacrifice of blood even greater.

159

Bibliography

The War Against Japan Major-General S W Kirby (HMSO, London)
The Battle of Matapan S W C Pack (Batsford)
Combined Operations 1940-1942 (HMSO, London)
The Campaign in Burma Frank Owen (HMSO, London)
The Transfer of Power in India V P Menon (London)
Burma Under the Japanese Thakin Nu (St Martin's Press, New York)
Defeat Into Victory Field-Marshall Viscount Slim (London)
The Two Viet-Nams Bernard B Fall (Praeger, New York)
The Last Years of British India Michael Edwards (London 1963)
Kogun, The Japanese Army in the Pacific War (US Marine Corps)
The Burma Front in Retrospect Major-General Hidegi Matsui (Kergokai, Tokyo)